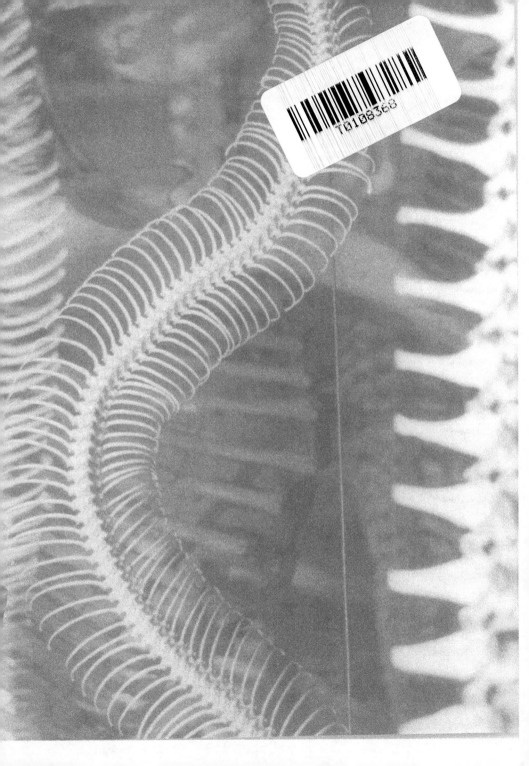

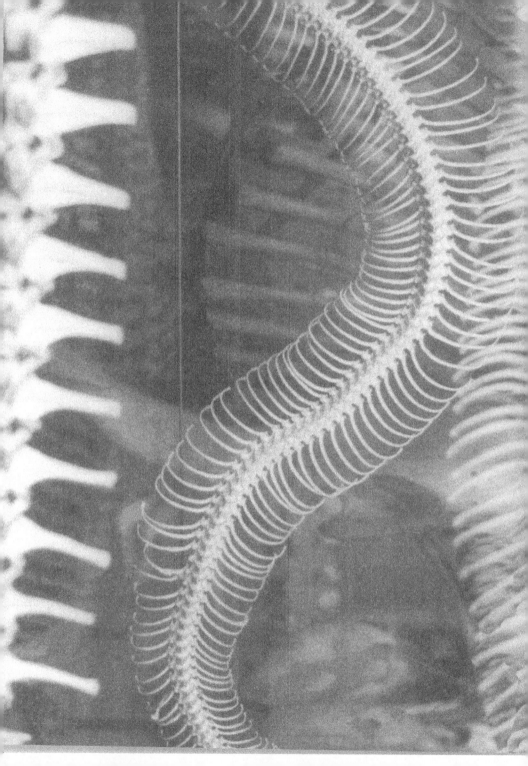

the monstrous
and the marvelous

the monstrous
and the marvelous

rikki ducornet

city lights
san francisco

Cover art: Ramón Alejandro
Cover design: Rex Ray
Endpapers: Photo by Jonathan Cohen
Book design: Elaine Katzenberger
Typography: Harvest Graphics

Library of Congress Cataloging-in-Publication Data

Ducornet, Rikki, 1943-
     The monstrous and the marvelous / by Rikki Ducornet.
          p.   cm.
     ISBN 0-87286-354-9 (pbk.)
     I. Title.
     PS3554.U279 M66   1999
     814'.54—dc21

City Lights Books are available to bookstores through our primary distributor:
Subterranean Company. P. O. Box 160, 265 S. 5th St., Monroe, OR 97456.
541-847-5274. Toll-free orders 800-274-7826. FAX 541-847-6018. Our books are
also available through library jobbers and regional distributors. For personal orders
and catalogs please write to City Lights Books, 261 Columbus Avenue, San
Francisco CA 94133. Visit our web site: www.citylights.com

CITY LIGHTS BOOKS are edited by Lawrence Ferlinghetti and Nancy J. Peters
and published at the City Lights Bookstore, 261 Columbus Avenue, San Francisco
CA 94133.

This book is for Nancy Joyce Peters
Grazie, creatura incantevole!

I search for an instant alive as a bird.
—Octavio Paz

TABLE OF CONTENTS

Waking to Eden   1

Optical Terror   7

The Impossible Genus   27

On Returning from Chiapas   33

Alphabets and Emperors   43

Optical Pleasure   53

Haunting by Water   61

Mapping Paris   65

The Monstrous and the Marvelous   69

The Death Cunt of Deep Dell   81

Sortilege   97

Books of Nature   103

A Dream   111

Manifesto in Voices   113

Acknowledgments   119

Bibliography   121

Abrecamino by Ramón Alejandro

WAKING TO EDEN

I was infected with the venom of language in early childhood when, sitting in a room flooded with sunlight, I opened an alphabet book. B was a Brobdingnagian tiger-striped bumblebee, hovering over a crimson blossom, its stinger distinct. This image was of such potency that my entire face — eyes, nose and lips — was seized by a phantom stinging, and my ears by a hallucinatory buzzing. In this way, and in an instant, I was simultaneously initiated into the alphabet and awakened to Eden.

In Eden, to see a thing Yahweh had dreamed and to say its name aloud was to bring it surging into the real. The letter B, so solid and threatening, *was* the bee; it was the embodiment of all its potencies. Looking at that letter, that blossom and that bee was like looking into a mirror from which the skin had been peeled away. The page afforded a passage — transcendental and yet altogether tangible.

Much later I learned that for the Kabalist, Beth is female and passive — a little house waiting to be prodded by the thrusting dart of letter A. Aleph, knowing that Beth will always be there, her door open in expectancy, boldly confronts the universe: O vigorous, confident, *thrusting* Aleph! (Now I know, too, just how *erotic* the image was — those engorged petals about to be ravished! Perhaps my sensuous life is here somehow reduced to its essential honey!)

Just as once Persian wizards read a sacred text on the bodies of tigers, I had, from that morning, entered into an exalted state from which I was never to entirely recover, expecting, no, *demanding* enchantment each time I opened a book. That letter B convinced me of what I think I already knew—that the world is a ceremonial dialogue to be actively engaged, and life's intention the searching out of the fertile passages and places, a fearless looking for the thorny A and B in everything.

A wood stretched behind the house; it was a place of wild hives, seed rattles, lost feathers, quartz fragments (and occasional arrowheads), and the gods themselves materializing in variable forms: horned beetle, red deer, fox, owl, snake (this was copperhead country), death's-head moth, hawk, hummingbird; stinkweed also, and a treacherous mud with a will of its own whose depth, in certain seasons, could not be determined. So many of the games I played there read now like rites of passage. I was very aware of danger—supernatural and actual; every time I penetrated into the wood I crossed a threshold from one cosmic dimension into another.

Each element of the wood implied a magical possibility; each element was, in fact, a potent letter, and all was contained—or so it seemed—in one vast *magic act*. I could not see a ladybug without entering into the ritual:

> *Ladybug, ladybug, fly away home!*
> *Your house is on fire! Your children have gone!*

It was here that I confronted death for the first time—in the shape of a fox, its inert body animated by a swarm of bees. I stood transfixed beside that vortex and knew *transformation* defines and rules the world. And because I had, in a room which now seemed worlds away, been myself changed forever by a letter in a book, I crouched and left a votive gift sublimely *transitional*, before moving on deeper into the world's wood—those gorgeous and terrifying images—like a necromantic alphabet of molten glass—pulsing behind my eyes.

the monstrous and the marvelous

I like to imagine that Adam's tongue, his palate and his lips were always on fire, that the air he breathed was kindled to incandescence each time he cried out in sorrow or delight. If fiction can be said to have a function, it is to release that primary fury of which language, even now, is miraculously capable — from the dry mud of daily use. So that furred, spotted and striped, it may — as it did in Eden — scrawl under every tree as revelation.

Language is magic — transforming dead snakes into animate nature. When language fails, as when memory fails, all we can hope for is an airless cabinet reeking of badly preserved specimens!

All my books investigate the end of Eden and the possibility of its reconstitution. I see them as Books of Nature and, because they are descriptive and painterly, as *vanitas* and *archetypa*, too. (I suppose, also, that because they all brood over singularities — ogresses, hunger artists, murderers and sirens — they could be said to fit into prodigy literature.)

My childhood heroes were Anton van Leeuwenhoek and Lewis Carroll; my ambition, never realized, to paint the museum scenery behind walruses and saber-toothed tigers. Even now I long for my own poetic territory which would include a keeping garden for insects, an extensive zoological library (color plates intact!), a wonder room and a jade cabinet which would, ideally, contain a chimera of mutton-fat jade.

And speaking of cabinets — I must admit that, despite a certain ambivalence (museums have all too often abetted the vanishment of species, as have botanical and zoological gardens) I am *glamourized* (charmed, in other words) by museums. Whenever I visit a new city, I get myself, just as soon as I can, to its museum of Natural History. In this way I have seen the bones of Brazilian sloths in Italy and Italian fossils in France. Museums recur in these essays not by choice but by inclination. This book, which was never intended to be one, is something like those early collections of miscellanea in which hedgehogs and astrolabes shared a shelf along with powdered mummy. The only ordering is what a Victorian might have called "the garden path of intuition." I see that some things resurge with persistence and of their own volition, such as babel towers, the word "delight," clocks, the Kabala, the idea (and the fear of) disorder, alphabets, and things in bottles.

I grew up in the Hudson Valley on the Bard College campus during the McCarthy era. Despite the times, it seemed safe, an enchanted place, almost tribal because of its isolated and intimate population. To my mind one of the campus' greatest pleasures was a bridge of green glass which led to the shelves of the library's second story: the room below appeared to be submerged in water. This bridge transformed a wonderful room into a veritable wonder room and the books I took home with me were *powers*. Whenever I crossed it, that bridge sparked a tremor of excitement; it is always a little frightening to walk on glass, even very thick glass. The bridge is still *un point de repère*: I am always looking for spaces which evoke a *sensation of strangeness* (Aragon's words), one that stimulates the eye, the imagining mind, and the body all at once. And a great museum, one that has not been banalized and overburdened by didactic concerns, does this.

But back to the bridge: imagine my delight when on a recent trip to Paris I visited the renovated Museum of Natural History's Grande Galerie de l'Évolution to discover that it is fitted out with glass bridges *and* glass elevators, so that the visitor and the specimens on display are all in suspension! The theme of the museum is this exactly: the suspension of life in space and time—that mystery, that vulnerability. *Be careful,* wrote Breton, *everything fades, everything vanishes . . .*

Everything here is seized in transparencies. Traveling from one floor to the next in a curiously vibrating glass box, one is startled by a band of monkeys climbing air and then: the stare of a sudden cockatoo. On the second floor flamingos rise from their cases as if to fly away or catch fire; below them a parade of large mammals flickers beneath a vastly accelerated day. (Later, dreaming my first psilocybin mushroom dream, I heard the words: *the insignificant instant signifies everything!*)

The Grande Galerie is at the far end of what was once the king's garden, a Wonderland garden, which has since blossomed into architecture of the most fertile sort, including a museum of minerals that houses a thicket of man-sized crystals budding and blossoming like plants, a museum of comparative anatomy containing a cyclopean cat, and a greenhouse where one may gaze at plants that mimic crystals. (The Grand Galerie offers animals that look like plants in mineral drag.) But now let's cross the river and visit the Louvre, and the model in miniature of Osiris' mummy, a planter, in fact, to be filled with soil and seeds so that the god may come to life again; and let's visit another room to see the faience figs belonging to the mummy of a queen, and a Horus carved of rock crystal.

I hope this collection will offer something of the excitement of such an aesthetic itinerary. And that these essays, more exactly *reveries*, will evoke some of the pleasure I have taken in gardens and museums and in the graceful spaces of other people's paintings, photographs, films, and books.

from *Physica Sacra Iconibus Illustrata* (1731–35) by Scheuchzer

OPTICAL TERROR

So many seas traversed!
—Francis Bacon

1. Cabinets of Marvels

The Enlightenment was preceded by the great voyages of discovery, which revealed a sprawling world, infinitely stranger than previously imagined. A World of Wonders reflected in *wunderkammern*, or cabinets of marvels in which the world's excess could be comfortably contained, as though so much savage and eccentric beauty — flamboyant birds, snakes broad as chimneys, pigs castellated with scales — could be assimilated in homeopathic doses only.

The fantastic influx of curiosities had a profoundly unsettling effect upon pedestrian and pious minds persuaded that the finite world was created reasonably, to the measure of man and for his salvation. Those Nest-building men of the woods, so like human parodies with their de Bergerac noses and scatological habits, must have badly cracked the egos of those who flattered themselves made in God's image. If people looked like God and *Semnopithecus nasica* like clownish men, then God had a little of the monkey and the universe was illumed as much by monkeyshine as votive candles. *Man lost his tail through friction and dis-use* saith Lord Monbodo. Darwin is just a sneeze away.

The insult culminates in Jonathan Swift's Yahoo—that fecal animal which would cure its own evil by eating its own shit, a practice popular in Swift's day (if no longer) and—as insalubrious as it undoubtedly was—still safer than the cosmetic use of white lead.[1]

If the intention of the *wunderkammern*[2] was to delight and instruct, the cabinets—and by extension botanical gardens and the first museums—are topsy-turvy and promiscuous. They reveal an existential stance, an Alchemy in Reverse. Here the natural world is ordered in ideal display, ideal because isolated and disaffiliated from the real. As beautiful as these collections often were, they betrayed a rupture at the heart of things and revealed a wound that has never ceased to fester, a chronic blindness also, an incapacity to read not only the New World's body, but its metaphysical books of days and dreams and prophesies. (I am thinking in this instance of the painted books of the Mexica reduced to ashes.) It is as if God gave man a second chance at Eden, and man, that confirmed shopkeeper, could not dwell there but only sell there.

Columbus returned to Spain with an ambulant cabinet of *naturalia* and *mirabilia* and so made an encyclopaedic entry into Barcelona with parrots and painted Indians. The Indians were not the teratological

---

1. An attempt to defy Time, the lead mask precipitated it, proposing an accelerated perspective:
    To see her from her pillow rise
    All reeking in a cloudy steam,
    Cracked lips, foul teeth, and gummy eyes,
    Poor Strephon, how he would blaspheme!
        ("The Progress of Beauty")
2. The influence of the cabinets is still evident today in the surviving museums of the eighteenth and nineteenth centuries. I am thinking of the singular scramble served up in a Parisean *rez de chausée* entitled *Anatomie Comparée* that includes the skeletal remains of Siamese twins (three-legged, they share a unique pelvic basin), a horned pig, and the penis of an elephant displayed in paper-thin slices. (These objects, of singular and tragic potency, appear briefly in my novel *Entering Fire*, City Lights 1986, 1999.)
    Niagara Falls' porous Barnum Museum (the last time I was there it was raining and I had to carry an open umbrella as I wandered the rooms) offers a mummy known as "the general," a bogus two-headed calf, and in a script of coleoptera glued to parchment, the words "Home Sweet Home" badly compromised by mites.

horrors previously imagined, but in his words *fair in limb, comely* and *well made*. Some were sent to Paris and given skirts provided by the Opéra; at least one was chained to a perch. Stolen from a world that burned as they were made to dance, the Indians were reduced to *lusus naturæ* clowning for kings.

~

Which brings us to the confirmed fool of fortune, Gulliver, marooned in countries that float on water or in the air, are lost in limbo like the scattered pieces of nursery puzzles, and perceived through lenses reductive, magnifying, fractured, and hot: Swift's eye cooks the world down to bone and lime.

In Brobdingnag, Gulliver as *nanunculus* is given a series of cabinets, the most hospitable conceived and executed by the royal cabinet maker, and supplied with a closet. A wee curiosity, Gulliver performs the favorite tricks of automata—drinking and fencing—and evokes Sade's captives in Silling, reduced to clockworks, chamber pots, and cream pitchers, and performing in fixed tableaux—diminished but for their ubiquitous genitals and anuses. (In this way Sade and his encyclopaedic schemes produce Wonder Rooms of another kind.)

In Lilliput, the entire world is reduced to the miniatures so favored in cabinets, and offers an Edenic space shimmering with gardens and toy cities like the brightly painted sets of cardboard theaters. The "Man-Mountain" Gulliver tumbles among the faultlessly pretty people like a bloated corpse from a coffin or a monstrous baby from its crib. Incapacitated and needy, swaddled with rope, he is Appetite personified, a natural catastrophe, the very Body of Corrupt Nature. Volcanic, he causes a hot wind, exudes a pestilential weather, produces downpours and mud slides. He is *Hekinah degul*, a vomitous kin and a hex who bites off far more than can be disposed of (an emblem for our times). If he is something of a famished eye in Brobdingnag, here he is more a raging anus. And he is an idol of sorts, closeted in a temple already polluted by an unnatural act—the murder that foretells his own plotted assassination. (The unthinkable size of his own virtual cadaver saves him.)

Murdering propriety, Gulliver leaves his dreadful droppings as deep in the dark as he can, thus transforming a temple into a water closet.

> But this was the only time I was ever guilty of so uncleanly an action ... From this time my constant practice was, as soon as I rose, to perform that business in open air, at the full extent of my chain, and due care was taken every morning before company came, that the offensive matter should be carried off in wheel-barrows ...

And when he saves the royal apartments from fire, his urine, too hot to handle, anticipates sexual scandal. If Gulliver is far too big to mate with Flimnap's wife (his rival is a light sleeper, one supposes), the *idea* of such a coupling is intolerable, a heresy illumed by Strephon's lust for Chloe (see Swift's peculiar poetry, so riddled with rage):

> ... *Can such a deity endure* [Chloe, thus far, and like the Lilliputians, has been seen from a distance, only.]
> *A mortal human touch impure?*
> ("Strephon and Chloe")

Chloe has taken twelve cups of tea, and by pissing proves that she is Strephon's size.[3] A potential corpse, as is he, she may be fucked,

---

3. *Distortions, groanings, strainings, heavings* . . . like Rabelais' Gargamelle's, Chloe's leavings are prodigious too. . . . But: is she shitting or giving birth? One thinks of Freud's little Hans, for whom all babies were "lumfs" and "born like lumfs." And Ambroise Paré's *Examples of Monstrous Things*, his tales of impostures, unforgettable and obscene, such as *The Woman who Pretended to have a Canker in her Breast* and the *Fat Wench from Normandy Who Pretended to have a Snake in her Belly.* Paré's *Example of Winds* is written in a manner that can only be called Swiftian with its descriptions of women whose bellies house colonies of frogs and whose percussive capacities are likened to artillery.

the monstrous and the marvelous

after all. Yet as she pisses, she expands; as does Gulliver in Lilliput *she fills the eye*. In fact, Chloe keeps on growing, until she belongs to the same race as the strapping wenches of Brobdingnag. Unmanned, Strephon chooses not to fuck her, but instead to *Let fly a rouser in her face.*

∾

In Brobdingnag, Gulliver is reduced to dependent infancy, bringing to mind the dwarves once kept by kings in miniature apartments. Like Sebastiano Biavati on display in a museum, he has his own wee chairs, china, and cutlery. In the minds of the *virtuosi*, he is an aborted embryo—a gnostical conceit that swells to the extreme distortions of anamorphic pictures in the country of the Houyhnhnms, where, among the perfunctory and impervious horses, the evidence against the Yahoos is absolute.

Gulliver as *nanunculus*, in cabinets padded, furnished, pierced with windows and more or less secure, is the great, great grandfather of Gregor Samsa, of Lucky, the Fly Man, and Charlie the tramp. His cabinets are the emblems of captivity and impotence, the Cathar's "filthy inn." Like Charlie, Gulliver is forever out of sync with his surroundings, his physical needs are flamboyantly in evidence: he is hungry, lonely, wanting to take a crap and his clothes don't fit. He is one helpless, fetal mistake among the many that abound in the Swiftian universe. The *Journal to Stella* is truffled with the fetal issues of lady friends—brats Swift would gladly see dead. Borges says it all in his marvelous tale of his imagined Orbis Tertius: *Mirrors and copulation are abominable because they increase the number of men.* (In passing, the *nanunculus* reappears in fetal state in Walpole's *Hieroglyphic Tales*: a royal twin, miscarried and bottled, is accidentally swallowed by an archbishop suffering colic.)

∾

If in Lilliput, Gulliver's mouth and anus are impossible to escape, in Brobdingnag the *nanunculus* is more a mouth, the suckling of a nurse, a frolicsome maid of honor, and a mischievous monkey whose perilous nursing brings King Kong's abduction of Fay Wray to mind. Having kidnapped Gulliver (Swift, too, was abducted by a nurse), the monkey proceeds to rock him and to cram his mouth with stuff he squeezes from his chops—and this three hundred yards from the ground.

Perilous feedings abound. Clearly, the Queen is capable of swallowing the little fetus whole and indeed, soon after the horrible ceremony of the Queen's dinner, Gulliver is dropped in cream. (The onomatopoetic *splacknuck* foretells of this near disaster.) Crammed into a hot marrow bone, he is reduced to stuffing. Once again, the argument is a gnostic one; Swift's act of inflation transforms something as banal as nursing a baby or eating dinner into a cosmic catastrophe.

Swift once ate one hundred apples at one sitting. (*Eating*, writes Norman O. Brown, *is the form of the fall.*) He blamed his dizzy spells, the ringing in his ears, on this single act of gluttony.

2. Laputa and Other Islands of the Mind

When in Brobdingnag Gulliver's cabinet is taken into the air by an eagle and dropped into the sea, he is saved by a ship's captain, to whom he reveals his collection of curiosities. These humble if oversized artifacts—a comb contrived from the stumps of the King's beard, four wasp stings, a corn from a maid of honor's toe and a footman's tooth—gently mock the optical babel of the Muse Rooms, and evoke, to my mind at least, Peter the Great's weakness for pulling other people's teeth. (The Tsar's ordering of little bones numbered and secured with ribbon, looks very like the calcified miters of a Lilliputian papality.) Still something of a curiosity himself, Gulliver informs the good captain that his breeches are made of the skin of a mouse.

Later, when Gulliver sets foot on Laputa, he carries but four

the monstrous and the marvelous

things: *flint, steel, match and burning-glass*. Compare this neat list with Crusoe's Universal Inventory of (Nearly) Everything; if Gulliver's excretory capacity once caused havoc in Lilliput, Crusoe hoards with compulsive anality:[4]

> *biscuit, liquor, silver and gold,*
> *five or six gallons of rack;*
> *powderhorns, shot, two rusty swords,*
> *clothes and a great screw jack.*
> *A large bag of shot,*
> *a hogshead of bread,*
> *a hammock, muskets and charts;*
> *dials, perspectives, several parcels,*
> *some bedding, good knives and forks.*
> *Some very good Bibles,*
> *pens, ink and scissors,*
> *spare canvas and all the ship's sails;*
> *a great roll of sheet-lead,*
> *three or four compasses,*
> *powder horns, two rusty swords.*
> *Money! And paper—*
> *drawers full of razors,*
> *cables, a howser*
> *two saws, an axe;*
> *a small sack of powder,*
> *one dog,*
> *two cats . . .*

Long and hopeful, Crusoe's list is a mingled *Mass of Things*, inadequate and incomplete. It cannot conjure order out of chaos, nor banish Death's shadow, that shadow Swift teases with terror and impropriety.

---

4. The list is long; the rhyme is mine.

~

Let's engage a reverie on Swift's sky-island Laputa, before evoking other islands of the mind. Floating above the confines of weather and common sense, Laputa, populated by cuckolds and eager whores, defies gravity as it reveals the nature of the Swiftian nightmare—so like Kafka's—in which tyranny is a palpable stuff, a pestilence and a pollution, corrupting the brain, the air, the eye. "High" Laputa navigates in a worldly stench: *Steams from Dunghills, Exhalations and a Smoak from Fire,* and is ruled by self-deluded Egg Heads who, having embraced lunacy as eagerly as their wives embrace strangers, live in the very "eclipse" with which they threaten Balnibarbi.

> *If any town should engage in rebellion or mutiny, fall into violent factions, or refuse to pay the usual tribute, the king hath two methods of reducing them to obedience. The first and the mildest course is by keeping the island hovering over such a town, and the lands about it, whereby he can deprive them of the benefit of the sun and the rain, and consequently afflict the inhabitants with dearth and diseases. . . . But if they still continue obstinate, or offer to raise insurrections, he proceeds to the last remedy, by letting the island drop directly on their heads. . . .*

As you will recall, the Laputans need flappers to function in the real; their bladders are filled with pebbles, or *pease,* and their conversation is as flat as porridge. No wonder their vivacious wives prefer to be "below" and in the company of vile footmen who, despite deformity, have both feet on the ground.

The Laputans live like *nanunculi* in constant fear of being *absorbed or swallowed up,* not by a Royal Body but a Celestial One: the approaching sun.

When I was your age I thought every day of death, Swift once wrote to Pope, *but now every night.* This is the terror of the Mad Hatter and the March Hare who also live a timeless distillation, having reduced their lives to the floating world of a perpetual tea party beneath the shadow of the Red Queen's axe. Orbiting the table, the Hatter and the Hare are able to forget Time (and so, mortality), just as the Laputans, lost in abstractions, may forget their own (and their wives') mortal (and sexual) selves. The shoddy world is always second best, and to flourish the eye needs the *Assistance of Artificial Mediums (A Tale of a Tub)*. In fact, like things in bottles, the creatures of Laputa might as well be blind:

> *Their heads were all reclined either to the right or left; one of their eyes turned inward, and the other directly up to the zenith.*

Dinner in Laputa is worthy of a Wonder Room feast:

> *In the first course, there was a shoulder of mutton, cut into an equilateral triangle, a piece of beef cut into a rhomboides, and a pudding into a cycloid. The second course was two ducks, trussed up into the form of fiddles; sausages and puddings resembling flutes and haut-boys, and a breast of veal in the shape of a harp. The servants cut our bread into cones, cylinders, parallelograms, and several other mathematical figures.*

If this fanciful meal evokes the eighteenth century's delight in encyclopaedic orderings, it also serves as a *vanitas*: those paintings of worldly delights—oysters, oranges and mandolins—in which a fly may be seen crawling over a slice of cheese, or about to drown in a glass of wine. The Laputans, after all, despite their fastidious orderings, do not *sleep quietly*.

3. Brainstorming

Among the word peddlers of the Grand Academy of Lagado, what Swift's friend Bishop Berkeley calls "sensible things" have become nonsensical; in such an extravagant language of utensils, artifacts and goods, there would need to be a unique object for each unique thing: eggs, teacups and yesterday's jam, not to mention kings, the concept of beheading, the rules for chess, sunbeams, walruses, and cabbages.

> . . . *since words are only names for* things, *it would be more convenient for all men to carry about them such things as were necessary to express the particular business they are to discourse on.* . . . *I have often beheld two of those sages almost sinking under the weight of their packs, like pedlars among us* . . .

According to Berkeley, the visible and tangible world is an enigma to be interpreted, a Divine Book to be read without False Lights. Clarity of vision is a moral necessity, and the cumbersome tokens of Lagado's virtuosi another version of the *Tubs'* Varnished Tinsel—seductions that divert man from the Truth.

The brainstorming laboratories of the Academy swarm with *feather-cutters,* monomaniacs ruled by *idées fixes.* The word *projector* conjures magic lanterns, Plato's cave, Berkeley's idealism, and even Signor Aldrovandi, the Bolognese Aristotle who attempted to order a Universal History of Everything. (Aldrovandi's special inquiry was into fetal chickens.) If the Academicians illustrate what Berkeley calls *the tragic folly of minds busy . . . from vain researches,* their skulls are yet another sort of cabinet rattling with fetal thoughts, teratological thoughts. Lagado illustrates the acute irony of this sentence from Swift's *Tub: We are to be thankfull for madness because it causes conquests and systems.*

Lagado's most sinister Academician is the physician whose cure for colic causes a dog to implode. An instance that recalls Hogarth's *Four Stages of Cruelty:* here boys are shown to torture animals in ways including: the suspension of cats by their tails, the piercing of a bird's eye with a burning stick, and the thrusting of an arrow up the anus of an immobilized dog. Beneath the scene, Hogarth has inscribed a poem. The first stanza reads:

the monstrous and the marvelous

> *While various Scenes of sportive Woe*
> *The Infant Race employ,*
> *And tortured Victims bleeding Shew*
> *The Tyrant in the Boy.*

Hogarth and Swift both demonstrate the savagery not only of the "Infant Race" but of a science that, to use a phrase of Berkeley's, *wanders through wild mazes* and finds justification in the phantasmal promise of progress. A lover of rational thinking, Swift is not trashing scientific inquiry but excess, bad faith and criminal foolishness. If man is capable of Reason (and, reasonably, Bishop Berkeley would have all inquirers *return to the simple dictates of nature*), he is not always (and not often) reasonable. Elsewhere Swift writes:

> *How I want thee, humorous Hogart*
> *Thou I hear, a pleasant rogue art;*
> *were you and I acquainted,*
> *Every monster should be painted.*
> *You should try your graving tools*
> *on this odious group of fools.*
> (—"A Character, Panegyric")

Like Berkeley, Swift was interested in facts, not "fruitless disquisitions," "*supposed* facts and empty abstractions, which an irregular exercise of the imagination or *abuse of words* (italics, mine), had put into place."

The act of creation, writes Bishop Berkeley, *consists in God's willing those things should become perceptible. . . . Man is a thinking, active principle, that perceives, knows, works and operates about ideas that are revealed as continuously real.* In other words, if man is a perceiving medium, perception is the extension and completion of the act of creation. The world is dependent on Mind. Mind is the active principle that reveals the world as real. By denying his capacity to perceive with clarity, to think rationally, man reduces himself—and the choice is his—to Yahoo. Only a fool would subvert or ignore his inherent capacity to read the Book of Nature.

~

If, when visiting the Academy of Lagado, Gulliver enjoys a certain spectator's distance, the projectors are so close to their projects that they have come to personify them. The lonely inquirer into excrements who embraces Gulliver—*a compliment I could well have excused*—is as putrefacient as his matter of inquiry. He is like *other insects* which, born and educated in shit, have come to exemplify it. The spider rancher's brain, netted by *metaphysical cobweb problems* (*A Tale of a Tub*) is as knotted as the web he tends, and one easily imagines the febrile intensity of the man who has written a treatise on the malleability of fire. But most worrisome of all, more than the elaboration of marble pillows and naked sheep, is Swift's *universal artist* who would condense air *into a dry, tangible substance,* thus putting the entire Academy at risk, and everyone else besides.

Now we come to the Academy's great treasure: the projector of Speculative Learning's word scrambler. Surely inspired by Athanasius Kircher's[5] *Arca Glollotactica* (which by the manipulation of levers could translate words from one language into another), Lagado's linguistic Arc (or word abacus) is no more than a maddening Babel Tower contained within a Closet Shut. It prefigures Borges' infinite library of formless books housed in hexagonal rooms, hexagonal because *The idealists argue (they) are a necessary form of absolute space.* . . . This reference to idealism is not fortuitous; like Swift, Borges was deeply affected by the idealism of Bishop Berkeley.

---

5. For more on Kircher (and Aldrovandi) see Paula Findlen's marvelous *Possessing Nature.*

the monstrous and the marvelous

4. The Fecal Eye

Cabinets of curiosities, still popular well into the eighteenth century, provided a species of looking glass into worlds of wonder most often arranged in "ideal" and impossible configurations. Among the pieces of mummy and horned beetles are optical instruments; the microscope, for example, which revealed the unexpected monstrosity of such common things as the face of a fly or a flea. And there were optical games, the most fascinating being anamorphic paintings and prints, which could be perceived only with the help of a cylindrical mirror.

In his *Anamorphoses*, Jurgis Baltrušaitis offers the curious image of a monstrously distorted eye. Set before a cylindrical mirror, that eye is made to reconstitute itself. He took this image from *Récréations* by Charles Ozanam, a book that was wildly popular in the first half of the eighteenth century. And although this lugubrious eye—which brings nothing so much to mind as Salvador Dali's fried eggs and the roving eye of Bataille *père*[6]—was intended to be that of Cardinal Colonna, archbishop of Bologna, its purpose to illustrate, metaphorically, the redressment of lost souls, it shall serve us now as the metaphorical eye of Jonathan Swift, whose distortions always reveal more about the world than they conceal. *Gulliver's Travels* is a collection of verbal anamorphoses, its optical illusions the diversions of a *sensible* observer who, although Bolingbroke suggested it, refused to put on "philosophical spectacles." And just as Berkeley suggests that the flea we see beneath the lens of the microscope is not a new sort of thing but still a flea, so Swift's reply to Bolingbroke is: *Put on what Spectacles You please. Your Guinea's but a Guinea still.*

In Brobdingnag, Swift's magnifying eye seizes *horrible spectacles:* the cancer, the wen; above all the lice and *much better than those of an European louse through a microscope.* . . . It is likely Swift's eye was informed by Robert Hookes' engraving in the *Micrographia* (London, 1665) of a

---

6. In his appendix to *Historie de l'oeil*, Bataille explains that his obsession with the eye and urine has everything to do with his syphilitic father.

louse rendered monstrous by magnification, clinging for all its worth to an outsize human hair. Like Hookes and Hogarth, Swift proposes inflation as a way to the Truth. Swift's Truth being very dark indeed, the entire social fabric may be read as a map leading to a mass grave: *If I tell you there is a Precipice under you and that if you go forward you will certainly break your necks: if I point before your Eyes, must I be at the Trouble of repeating it every Morning? (A Tale of a Tub).*

Throughout the *Travels*, Gulliver is like one who gazes at a catoptric anamorphose and sees a skull and his own reflection in the same instant; he is both the fetus in the bottle and the eye gazing at it in fascination; the anus and the eye painted at the bottom of the chamber pot. His eye feeds not on light but on darkness; it is an eye probing a black hole for an answer that can only be an acute disappointment, an eye poised like Laputa in a stench. *I exist*, writes Bataille, *suspended from my own dread*. He could be speaking for Swift. This fecal eye also evokes Sade; the answer to the riddle *My tongue is black, my mouth is furred* is "Celia shits."

Last week I saw a woman flayed and you will hardly believe how much it altered her person for the worse! (The Correspondence). Among the passionless horses, it is Gulliver who is flayed, revealed to be a seething sewer, just as Beauty, *picking out a crystal eye* is revealed to be a potential cadaver. The unmasking is as convulsive as an abrasive purge. Just another Yahoo, Gulliver finds himself up to his chin in the primal ordure of his origins: *corrupted mud and slime . . . ooze and froth of the sea*. Hot and filthy, he is the product of the solar ovary and a seminal (and caustic) rain, yet so irresistible he causes the nubile Yahoo to howl with lust (one supposes Stella, on occasion, howled too). Flesh is chaos; telluric and volcanic it may erupt at any moment, as in Swift's poem "A Lady's Dressing Room":

> *When frightened Strephon cast his eye*
> *It showed the visage of a giant:*
> *A glass that can to sight disclose*

The smallest worm in Celia's nose,
And faithfully direct her nail
To squeeze it out from head to tail,
For catch it nicely by the head,
It must come out alive or dead.

The "worm" erupting from Beauty's face is just another form excrement takes when it is not raining from the hairy holes of Yahoos perched in trees, or falling from the sky as atomized bodies: *I had seen them blow up a hundred . . . at once . . . beheld the dead bodies come down in pieces from the clouds. . . .*

Writes Bataille:

> *And just as the freed obscene nature of their organs more passionately connects embracing lovers, so, too, the nearby horror of the cadaver and the present horror of blood, tie the one that dies more obscurely to an empty infinity—and this infinity is itself projected as a cadaver and as blood.*
>
> (*—Visions of Excess*)

∾

In Beauty's bed, appetite, copulation, birth, death and defecation are all contained in (and exemplified by) the vortex—and I use that word precisely because it best describes the vertiginous quality of Swift's vision, a vision informed by his chronic malaise: characterized by precipitous vertigo and severe unbalance, the world, in seizure, appears to spin. If the Grildrig[7] in Brobdingnag is in danger of being

---

7. The name given to Gulliver in Brobdingnag, *"Grildrig,"* is a rich portmanteau of provocative possibilities; *grig:* grasshopper, cricket, small eel; and grill and girl, of course. The outsized Queen drops her gold ring over Gulliver, girding and girdling him, and, one supposes, nearly getting rid of him. The Grildrig is something of a riddle also, as is his puzzling world.

rikki ducornet   21

swallowed whole by outsized vulvas, tumors, molehills and animals, the greediest orifice belongs to Time.[8]

In Swift's universe, Time is female; female flesh epitomizes dissolution. Returning at the witching hour of midnight, Corinna (*The Progress of Beauty*) sits on her three-legged chair—in other words, her bidet—and pulls off her hair and plucks out her eye. The passage of time accelerates to a dizzying degree; like particles in an atomic canon, matter fractures and dissolves. Corinna's macabre striptease reveals that she is in fact an upholstered coffin; tacks, tassels and padding removed, all that remains is an eager abyss. (*Eager* because once abed, the hag lies awake tormented by thoughts of love.)

Corinna's glass eye is a species of genital; it fits, after all, into an orifice and, with a glance can "glamourize"; like a phallus, pierce to kill. Just as cosmetics, *those ointments good for scabby chops (The Lady's Dressing Room)* mask the abuses of time, the eye fills the absence that contains it. Beauty is a corpse in drag, a sieve-woman riddled with holes. Magnified, her skin appears like a graveyard erupting pestilence. Sweat is a caustic, smelly substance, and love's fire *brings a stench from every pore (A Description of a Salamander)*. Corinna's eye socket is her glass eye's casket, her mouth a reliquary that contains her dead teeth, her body melted down to an anamorphic spill. But Swift's own eye is bigger than his stomach. Having taken on more than he can chew, he cannot swallow and so *will spew*.

Incapable of love, Swift cannot forgive the flesh because it dies; he cannot forgive womankind the transitory physicality that defines, determines and damns him, too. In his spyglass poems—those poems in which the masculine eye burglarizes the absent Beauty's chamber,

---

8. Perhaps the cacophony that tortured Swift's wounded inner ear translated into an exacerbated perception of the particulating world. Cossinus, that exemplary Swiftian hero, who having seen too much is undone, *scorched by the sight of Celia's horrid fact* ("Cossinus and Peter"). Whipped by scorpions, badly stung, he has seen the Medusa's face: her serpents hiss at him directly. (The other symptoms of Ménière's is tinnitus: a rumbling and hissing in the ears.)

peeping into the very things that cause virility to recoil, the distinction between the real and the false, corruption and health, sex and death dissolve and decay; these ravished rooms swell and crack as in the throes of intense seismic upheaval.

The descent into the female vortex culminates in the revelation of that *vile machine*, that *reeking chest*, Celia's own *Pandora's box*: her chamber pot which, as Groddeck proposes, when stained with menstrual blood, is for the little boy the proof that the female is a castrated male. Celia's own chamber pot, like a Brobdingnagian wench's vulva, is a metaphor for the Medusa herself: the look that turns a man to stone. It is no accident the Nanunculus grildrig's intimate view of a frolicsome girl's outsize cabinet of curiosities — a mirror of his own incapacities — is followed by a decapitation that in a fit of lyricism, Gulliver likens to the (ejaculating) fountains of Versailles.

Vulnerable when open and closed, the eye is a paradoxical organ. Unlike the stomach (or the mouth) it cannot give back what it has taken in. If a bad meal can be vomited or, with difficulty, digested, a horrific vision, repressed, is made to fester. Groddeck points out that the child first sees himself reduced and contained within the mother's eye.

Hot, nurturing, pregnant with the little child, the eye is not like the mother but *is* the mother. Magically it has diminished and imprisoned the child, like a dwarf in the palace of a Queen. If we are struck by something — as Strephon is struck by horror — the vision has pierced the eye and impregnated it with monsters.

This phallic eye is incarnated by Swift's "Salamander." A venomous fang, a poison pendulum: . . . *it spews a filthy froth, (whether through rage, or lust, or both) of matter purulent and white, which happening on the skin to light, And there corrupting to a wound Spreads a leprosy and baldness round.* The organ of self-perpetuating and self-punishing anger, the phallic eye is also very cold: *So cold, that put in the fire, 'twill make the very flames expire.* . . .

Throughout the *Travels* Gulliver devours with his eyes: the Queen of Brobdingnag's prodigious mouth, the breast tumor full of holes large enough to contain him, the Yahoo's filthy Excrements, hairless Anus and Pudenda. By tale's end he is stuffed to the point of gagging. It is not surprising that Swift insists upon the mouth, the genitals, and the anus, for they are emblematic of the body's dependency, a dependency that teaches the dark truth about a "Mother" Nature whose exigencies are absolute—"Truth" intolerable to a loveless and alienated spirit. (For it seems to me that the passage of time and the limitations of mortality are bearable, even acceptable, to those who dare engage in the world fully, and unbearable to those who do not. Recall how Swift's own "Saucebox" Stella was imprisoned in the airtight cabinet of a secret and sterile marriage.)[9]

Finally, in his poem "A Panegyric on the Dean," Swift's Queen of gluttony confines her daughter Cloacine to the outhouse where she gives birth to an *impious line* of Goddesses and Gods including *Voluptuous Ease*. Once again, a purposeful confusion is entertained between the mouth, the anus, and the womb. Cloacine's brood pay tribute to their mother in the form of turds, and Swift complains they do not leave them in nature. The *sincerest* turd is dropped by a peasant in a clay pot, or upon the humble branches of a bush—not into a silver vase by a Duchess. The bucolic turd is described with seeming tenderness (again bringing Sade to mind and those curious "ices" served at Silling): it has a spiral top, or a copple-crown. (When Sade proposes his encyclopaedic peep shows, he, too, is impossibly remote *and famished*—as though he hopes the sheer weight of excess will so gorge the eye it will, at last, be sated. When Beauty appears in Silling she is quickly smeared with dung or blood; pleasure depends upon the end of Beauty or, at the very least, her humiliation. When treated well

---

9. Did Swift marry Stella? There is a good chance he did, in order to *contain* her, yet never consummate the marriage.

the monstrous and the marvelous

she is buggered; it is the ass, in Silling, that catches the eye first and foremost.)

Shitting is the price we pay for being mortal, the ticket we hand to the Creator in order to participate in the spectacle that is the world. By insisting we shit in His garden, Swift may be asking we pay God in kind, to send, in the great tradition of clowns secular and holy, the pie soaring back into His face. After all, Swift might say: the trick He has played is a Dirty One.

Wax head of an albino man
Museo Césare Taruffi, Istituto di Anatomìa e Istologìa Patològica
Photograph by Rosamond Purcell

THE IMPOSSIBLE GENUS

In 1998, I visited St. Petersburg, eager, above all, to see Peter the Great of Russia's *kunstkammer*, and this because of his collection of anomalies prepared with loving eccentricity by Frederick Ruysch (1638–1731), the great Dutch anatomist, who shared with Peter a fascination with aberrations of the human form. My project demanded a certain degree of stubbornness because of the squeamishness of my Russian guides who feared the collection would leave an indelibly foul impression. Yet, as it turned out, Ruysch's curious parcels of matter suspended by wire in keeping medium have weathered far better in my mind than the creepy border guards (it took five hours to enter Russia from Estonia), archly grouchy hotel attendants, shrill *babushkas* and other scolds who were, during my brief stay, so much in evidence.

It is not easy to convey in words the extraordinary quality of human tenderness Ruysch's monsters communicate; the delicacy of his preparations offer an undeniable image of transcendence. While I was there, the gallery devoted to Ruysch was filled with awed children moved to quiet contemplation. A weird aesthetic is revealed in these eventful rooms: a baby white as ivory inwardly dreaming has limbs and neck circled with white and black beads; a little arm and hand, its fingernails carefully painted black by the anatomist's daughter, is served up on a white sleeve; an infant's perfect face floats like a lunar disc in a nimbus of lace. Despite the passage of the centuries, she has kept her rosy lips and cheeks, and one can well believe that Peter kissed those lips through the glass. Each of these catastrophes is as articulate as the blossoms of Alice's Wonderland.

Some of the specimens have pained expressions as though the burden of matter had been prematurely revealed to them by the singular commotion of their gestation. An infant in the stranglehold of the headless sibling soldered to its breast appears both exhausted and stunned; another, without eyes or nose, seems to sob. One gazes into their glass domiciles as a tortured soul must gaze into a mirror. Others, less terrible, lord over the place mutely, much as the fabulous gods of India that animate adjacent rooms.

~

The monstrous is unsettling because it appears to belong nowhere but its own boundless category. Like a lobster at a kosher meal, it always exemplifies chaos. Reduced to curiosities, the bearded lady, the piebald child and the dwarf are thrust into an impossible genus: *extraordinem* — containing everything from fingered lemons to bogus mermaids.

Peter's *Kunstkammer* claimed four human prodigies including a dwarf so prized that when he died Peter had him stuffed and placed on view along with all the other *meraviglie* including his defunct footman's seven-foot skeleton, topped by a skull that, mysteriously, was not his own. The seventeenth-century dwarf Sebastiano Biavati was the curator of the cabinet in which he was on display — a species of genteel house arrest — and was the only thing alive in a collection of tusks, dead turtles, corals and curious shells.

In her extraordinary *Special Cases: Natural Anomalies and Historical Monsters*, a book inspired by the exhibition of her work that she curated for the Getty Museum in 1994, Rosamond Purcell writes:

We always drive the monster out — to live beyond geographical boundaries of the known world, to be set out, figuratively upon the water as on a ship of fools, to be ostracized on the street, treated as insane, or as a singular being who truly has no group at all and who is forced to live like the Minotaur, Grendel, or Caliban — in a labyrinth, on the edge of town, or at the far end of the island.[1]

If the monster is made to live in banishment, his place of origin too, is that of exile: *Note that at the furthest reaches of the world often occur new marvels and wonders,* wrote the fourteenth-century author of the *Polychronicon, as though Nature plays with greater freedom secretly at the edges of the world than she does openly and nearer us in the middle of it.*

At the end of the eighteenth century, the French natural historian Buffon, eager to calculate "appropriate" human size, decided that the average height of a man was five feet, a giant seven, and a dwarf three. And if he conceded that the sizes of giants and dwarfs are variable, he was certain the ideal was constant at five. One cannot help but think of Dean Swift's vision of shrinking and expanding humanity, and one need not be a dwarf to sympathize with Gulliver's emblematic impotency and infantilization in Brobdingnag, nor to be incensed by Purcell's historical examples of sentient beings reduced to toys and the slavish objects of erotic games — such as the tiny cripples sold for pleasure in the specialized markets of Rome, or Joseph Bornuwlaski (1739–1837), admired by aristocrats for his wise and brilliant conversation, who suffered the Swiftian indignity of being dandled on the laps of great ladies. I imagine Mr. Bornuwlaski's famous "fiery eyes" burned very darkly indeed at such moments.

People, Purcell reminds us, *struggle to redefine their territories in order to better determine the "center" of the world and to declare who should occupy it.* Purcell's

---

1. Rosamond Purcell's photographs and installations have appeared all over the world in books, journals, and museum exhibitions. See also her recent collaboration with the naturalist Stephen Jay Gould in *Finders Keepers: Treasures and Oddities of Natural History, Collectors from Peter the Great to Louis Agassiz* (W. W. Norton, 1992).

intention is not merely to offer a glimpse of the world's *fantastic edges* (although her gorgeous photographs demonstrate no one behind a camera today "sees" those edges as she does) but to remind us that the informed heart encompasses all edges, imagined and unimaginable, known, unknown and knowable. The world is not threatened nor diminished but instead made richer by such marvelous beings as Mary Sabina, the astonishingly beautiful "Piebald Black Child" (born in 1736), whose portraits acquire an emblematic potency not because of her exotic environs, her skin so very black, so very white, but because the white mark on her black brow is in the shape of a dove in flight. Like the *signifying monkey* of the East that Purcell elsewhere describes, who delivers and interprets sacred messages, Mary Sabina is full of signifying ways. And it is no accident that having offered us this vision of transcendence, Purcell next evokes *black catching* in Tasmania (an activity that brought about the extinction of an entire human group) and quotes both Louis Agassiz and Anthony Trollop.

Says Agassiz:

> . . . *I experienced pity at the sight of this degraded and degenerate race, and their lot inspired compassion in me in thinking that they are really men. Nonetheless it is impossible for me to repress the feeling that they are not of the same blood as us.*

And Trollop:

> . . . *of the Australian black man we may certainly say that he has to go. That he should perish without unnecessary suffering should be the aim of all those who are concerned in the matter.*

This racism is all the more appalling in the context of her book, in which the boundaries of the human have been so usefully, so graciously extended.

⁓

the monstrous and the marvelous

Life can be monstrous, because it is born of and ends in chaos, but moral and existential dilemmas are not solved (and are often aggravated) by gathering and classifying. *Implied in the institutional hoarding of dead things,* Purcell writes, evoking in this reader the drugged denizens of our mental institutions, *is a shoring up against mortality.* In the Western world, personal pride has long been confused with ownership. And ownership, Purcell demonstrates, is always political. *Both the impulse and the achievement may be termed as monstrous.*

Rosamond Purcell's thoughtful study of anomalies closes with a picture of a human skeleton with its face in a book. We are reminded that even as the world totters towards the twenty-first century, the pursuit of forbidden knowledge is persistently perceived as heresy. Evocative of the wonder rooms and magic lantern shows of another age, Purcell's own imaginative act of subversion proposes we look closely at the mirror's other side. *In between the monstrous and ourselves,* Purcell writes,

> *we have constructed many walls. . . . Through the centuries Western scholars have cited hairiness, darkness, smallness, imperfect rational skills as justification for questioning the eligibility of those possessing these traits for membership in the human race. . . . The issue in the study of anomalies is always one of classification — of perspective, scale, and the deep, inherited "misseeing" of the anomalous fictional creature and the genuine anomalous human being, which goes on and on.*

Jennifer Miller, a contemporary "Bearded Lady" and a New Yorker who refuses to be victimized by her condition, calls herself a "transgressive performer." She says: *I live in a very liminal place. It is a lovely place. In the theater it's when the lights go out and before the performance begins.*

This is what Rosamond Purcell proposes: that when the lights go on and the "special case" appears before us, we dare share that liminal space and embrace the marvelous diversity of what the great dreamer of monstrosity Jorge Luis Borges called: *The unique human species.*

Daigne agréer cette jeune et douce compagne ; elle est sensible, elle t'aimera.

"Deign to welcome this young and sweet companion;
she is sensible, and she will love you."

ON RETURNING FROM CHIAPAS:
A REVERY IN MANY VOICES

1. The One Pearl

In this country everyone dreams. Now the time has come to awaken . . .
—Subcomandante Marcos
from "Two Winds: A Storm and a Prophecy"

Iranian Gnosticism offers an exemplary text called *The Hymn of the Pearl*. It proposes the mystical itinerary of a king's son who, like Christ, makes his way down into the world in order to recover the One Pearl from the depths of the sea. The sea is in fact our world submerged in a drunken sleep, and the One Pearl represents the soul. It is guarded by a serpent—not the serpent that offered gnosis to Adam and Eve, but chaos: that venomous principle.

The searcher's itinerary takes him first to Babel—there where the muddling of tongues confounds the cause of brotherhood—and then to Egypt, the land of black earth and alchemy. There he is made to drink the wine of sleeping and forgetting. He comes to resemble his captors; without a quest he is a slave. But then a letter from "home" arrives—a summons to awakening. It is a call to being, the gnostical calling forth of the sleeper's innate capacity for becoming. Not surprisingly, the words of the letter mirror the words that are written on the seeker's heart. They rouse him from his slumber and illumine his path. Empowered, he charms the serpent and claims what is his.

To continue a moment longer with gnostic metaphors, recall how Kafka's Barnabas—*the only messenger sent to K*—is himself the message. The message, the wakening call, is love, love in what may be its most selfless form: brotherhood. If what is written on the pearl seeker's heart is his own innate capacity for moral being and his only chance for transcendence, Barnabas is K's only chance for being truly human. This is why *The Castle* is such a tragic book. K is blind, incapable of reading into his own heart, incapable of seeing that Barnabas is his brother.

Kafka's vision of a corrupt, frenzied, and unjust world was precipitated and informed by his own father's extensive holdings and brutal treatment of those in his service. (He once threatened to bone his son like a fish.) In fact, the Kafka microcosm very neatly mirrors industrialized Czechoslovakia. A self-congratulatory, self-perpetrating patriarchy, racist, classist, and burdened with acute social, economic, and political contradictions, Kafka's Czechoslovakia is emblematic of a modern and universal predicament.

Which brings us to Mexico. Exemplary castle of the Third World in crisis, it is here, at the end of this most tragic of centuries, that a voice resonates like a call to being: *When the storm subsides, when the fire and rain leave the earth in peace once again, the world will no longer be the world but something better* (Subcomandante Marcos). And it is here that a grassroots revolution is taking place of international significance: *The uprising coincided with the enactment of the North American Free Trade Agreement. The Zapatista army called NAFTA "a death sentence for Indians," a gift for the rich that will deepen the divide between narrowly concentrated wealth and mass misery, destroying what remains of their indigenous society* (Noam Chomsky). *We were going to enter into NAFTA like Christ with all his beggars and sit happily at the banquet; or was the United States contemplating the inclusion of the indigenous people into the trade agreements? There are more than 6.4 million Indians in our country* (Elena Poniatowska).

~

Fostered in the name of national unity and national pride, and founded on tribal prejudice and the law of exclusion, NAFTA brings nothing so much to mind as Kafka's take on Babel, the Great Wall of China, that dogma full of holes. The extreme alienation of the Mexican people, half of whom live below subsistence level, is shared by the dispossessed all over the planet—dispossessed of historical context, of cultural integrity, of a past, a future, of dignity, of landscape: *[They] saw forests being cut down to become supports for the wall, saw mountains being hewn into stones for the wall* (Kafka). However, the struggle goes back to the time of the conquest: *The machine that Christopher Columbus hammered into shape . . . was a kind of . . . medieval vacuum cleaner. The flow of nature . . . was interrupted by the suction of an iron mouth, taken thence through a transatlantic tube to be deposited and redistributed in Spain* (Antonio Benítez-Rojo).

Listen to the testimony of one of the New World's rare travelers who had the courage to remain wide awake:

The pearl fishers dive into the sea at a depth of five fathoms, and do this from sunrise to sunset, and remain for many minutes without breathing, tearing the oysters out of their rocky beds where the pearls are formed. They come to the surface with a netted bag of these oysters where a Spanish torturer is waiting in a canoe or skiff, and if the pearl diver shows signs of wanting to rest, he is showered with blows, his hair is pulled and he is thrown back into the water, obliged to continue. . . . At night the pearl divers are chained so they cannot escape (Bartolomé de Las Casas).

> *. . . they go toward*
> *a sea without its dawns*
> *those who hide their hunched backs*
> *those who hide burns under shawls*
> *those who weep when they hear music*
> *those who weep when drinking water*
>   (—Ambar Past)

2. These Things Happen

I don't know
in the mountains
these things happen
     (—Mónica Mansour)

Beyond a certain point there is no return. This point has to be reached.
    (—Franz Kafka)

    I returned recently, with three friends (Anne Waldman, Andrew Schelling, and Jonathan Cohen), from San Cristóbal de Las Casas, there where Bartolomé de Las Casas was briefly bishop. The present bishop, Samuel Ruíz García, has a profound and engaged respect for the people of his diocese, the dispossessed Maya of Chiapas: *We have to be on the side of those who are suffering the most,* he told an interviewer. *We found ourselves needing to build an authentic church.* Just like those who have taken up arms in order to live, Bishop Ruíz is a *professional of hope.* In a political context in which people are reduced to slaves and land to raw materials for industrial exploitation, in which laws are determined by markets and not by the demands of justice, and markets by profits and not by the essential needs of the people, the idea of brotherhood is a subversive idea. As does Barnabas in the land of the Castle, Bishop Ruíz threatens the oppressive system in place, an economic system of such violence that, as Subcomandante Marcos describes it, *one and a half million people have no medical services at their disposal . . . 54 percent of the Chiapan population suffers from malnutrition. . . . Education? The worst in the country . . . of every one hundred children, seventy-two do not finish first grade.* Says Ruíz: *It should be fully understood that the Kingdom of God is not constructed in eternity, although it ends there, but that it is built here, starting with the poor, that is what Jesus preached.*

    The paradox at the heart of Christianity is palpable in Chiapas where the Catholic Church—historically the prime oppressor—is represented by a bishop whose teachings include the Mayan Book of Creation—

36   *the monstrous and the marvelous*

*Pain! That's all you've done for us. Our mouths are sooty, our faces are
sooty.*
By setting us on fire all the time you burn us.
    (—the cooking pots speak in the *Popol Vuh*)

—and a bishop who knows the fight for human dignity is not only
spiritual and existential, but economic and political. In Ruíz's hands
the Church has become (and for this he is risking his life) an animat-
ing and a liberating force. *I care little for theology,* says Ruíz; *what's
important is liberation,* words that bring to mind the great *campesino* revolutionary Emiliano Zapata, who proposed that tyranny is overthrown
not on the battlefield alone but by *hurling ideas of redemption.*

    Everything is red, I tremble. The phantoms of fright, of
    the great fear, boil in my mouth.
        (—David Huerta, from "Incurable")

    In 1992, what remained of the communal lands from the land
reforms of the 1930s under Cárdenas were converted into salable
properties to facilitate Mexico's entry into NAFTA. Many farmers
were forced to sell the land that sustained them.

    Here you are dispossessed
    and belong to the nothing of nobody
        (—Kyra Galván, from "City Woman")

    The Maya have pushed deeper into the forests in order to plant
their crops of corn, beans, and coffee. On the road to San Cristóbal we
saw corn growing along the steep flanks of the mountain among rocks.
Some trees left standing are trimmed of branches taken for firewood. The
eroded soil reddens the roads to San Andrés Larrainzar, to Zinecantán.
San Juan Chamula, Chenalhó. This claiming of forest is born of necessity; the Men and Women of Corn—the Tzeltales, Tzotziles, Ch'oles,
Tojolabales, Zoques, Mames, Zapotecos, and Lacandóns —are starving,

their children so weakened they die of whooping cough and measles. The poet Ambar Past, who publishes *La Jicara*—one of the world's loveliest literary journals—in San Cristóbal, told us: *The winter I arrived here, all the children of the nearby village of Magdalenas died. All the children died.*

> *The dead come to us when we're dreaming*
> (—Ambar Past, from "The Sea on Its Side")

1984: Mexico City
The Resurrection of the Living

The Mexicans make a custom of eating death, a sugar or chocolate skeleton dripping with colored caramel. In addition to eating it, they sing it, dance it, drink it, and sleep it. Sometimes, to mock power and money, the people dress death in a monocle and frock coat, epaulettes and medals, but they prefer it stripped naked, racy, a bit drunk, their companion on festive outings.

Day of the Living, this Day of the Dead should be called, although on reflection it's all the same, because whatever comes goes and whatever goes comes, and in the last analysis the beginning of what begins is always the end of what ends.

"My grandfather is so tiny because he was born after me," says a child who knows what he is talking about. (Eduardo Galeano)

∾

In Mexico, poetry and revolution join hands, and Bishop Ruíz is only one messenger in a land that crackles with signification. Says Elsa Cross, a poet who is also a philosopher of religion: *Poetry is the foundation of the self through the world . . . a constant perception, an inner sound, a way of loving life.* Writes David Huerta: *Now, writing is a form of the body* (from "Incurable").

the monstrous and the marvelous

3. Let's Suppose

> Let's suppose a zone of the world falls together
> from Atlantic to Pacific,
> from Portugal to Japan,
> from the Mediterranean to the North Sea
> to the eastern Arctic.
> Let's suppose strange myths lift
> from the ancient caves of Altamira
> and the ruins of Turkistan,
> something like Viking ships
> and fresh legends of Tartars and samurai.
> Let's suppose the Yankee government doesn't please them
> and they decide to destabilize it.
>   (—Elena Milán, from "Hallucination I")

In the early evenings of winter, the city of San Cristóbal mists over; we were there late summer and each afternoon watched the rain clouds gather, the weather forming. The streets, many paved with stone, some of earth, are deep; we easily imagined those streets filled with rushing water during the season of rain. And we imagined the streets—streets in which Tzeltal, Tzotzil, Ch'ol, Tojolabal, Zoque, and Lacandón are spoken—filled with Comandante Ana María's freedom fighters come down from the mountains to declare war: *Today we say Basta ya!*

To our surprise, we found out there were Indian women among the leaders of the EZLN in the Lacandón jungle. Women who led battalions and gave orders in a clear, unflinching voice, women called Ramona, Petra, Ana María, Jesusa, Chabela, Amalia. Women who did not know how to read and write and who did not speak Spanish. . . . All of them looked like Rigoberta Menchú except for the fact that they did not wear beautifully embroidered blouses and sashes, nor did they knit ribbons into their thick black braids, but carried two bandoliers of cartridges over their shoulders and a gun strapped onto their hips. These women were hidden away in the muddy trenches in a mountain pass, or behind a red bandanna. Anonymous women were leading an army of two thousand Zapatistas (Elena Poniatowska).

The resurgent capacity of the collective memory of the Maya was now tested and proven: despite five hundred years of systematic violence, it served as a force for liberation and a source of self-determinism. Writes Elaine Katzenberger: *Public sympathy for the Zapatistas was immediate and overwhelming. Demonstrators filled plazas throughout the country—and in many foreign cities as well—holding banners that read, "We are all Chiapanecos." It soon became apparent that the government would be forced to acquiesce to the growing international demand for a cease-fire. A sense of shared triumph began to spread. On the day that the official cease-fire was declared, there was a large demonstration in Mexico City. Over 100,000 people marched together shouting "First World, HA HA HA!"* It was as though K had dared storm the Castle and rudely rouse Herr Klamm from his slumber. *We do not receive any help from foreign governments, persons or organizations. We have nothing to do with narco-trafficking or national or international terrorism. We are tired of years of abuse, lies and death. We have the right to fight for our lives and dignity. We have at all times obeyed international laws in war respecting the civil population* (Subcomandante Marcos, from "A Message to North America").

Marcos does not see himself as the leader of the Maya, but in their service, and in the service of a great idea: the idea of dignity. In other words, Marcos is not interested in ideology in the same way Ruíz is not interested in theology. In this unique revolution, ideology and theology have been usurped by a passion for liberty. Which makes for the most *poetical* of revolutions—one that André Breton would surely have applauded for its *convulsive beauty*. In his justly famous "Two Winds: A Storm and a Prophecy" (August 1992, published in *La Jornada* 27 January 1994), Marcos manages not only to give a concise map of the crushing exploitation of Chiapas, but to offer a vision of renewal. More than a response to tyranny, more than a list of grievances, more than a demand that essential needs be met, and swiftly, "Two Winds" is a summons, a message of urgency rising

the monstrous and the marvelous

from a dying world, a wakening call: *This wind will blow from the mountains born under the trees and conspiring for the new world, so new that it is scarcely an intuition in the collective heart it animates.*

> *The world tells me what has to be. There is a living flame.*
> *I shall have to say what I must say — or be silent.*
> (—David Huerta, from "Incurable")

> *Repeated to the end of centuries*
> *it vibrates in the ear of stone . . .*
> (—Elsa Cross, from "Canto Malabar")

∾

Before ending, I wish to return, briefly, to Kafka, whose fictions illumine an inevitability: hatred or indifference of the Other (and indifference is just one of hatred's many faces) leads to a sickness of the heart. Among the many examples Kafka offers is the figure of Pallas in the fable "A Fratricide." From his balcony, Pallas silently observes a murder; he does nothing to stop it, although a cry from him would suffice. Once the corpse lies bleeding in the street, Pallas is filled with self-loathing and *chokes on the poison in his body.* Else the world be the black mirror of Kafka's darkest premonitions, let us look to Mexico, and let us listen: *A wind rises up and everything is resolved. He rises up and walks to meet with others. Something tells him that his desire is the desire of many and he goes to find them* (Subcomandante Marcos, from "Two Winds," *Voice of Fire*).

> *What, then? My feet call to me with a deep tenderness, a*
> *pair of neutral feet, terrestrial; feet of a human being,*
> *pieces of single and doubled flesh, feet of deep and*
> *hopeful walks.*
> (—David Huerta, from "November Rain,"
> *Light from a Nearby Window*)

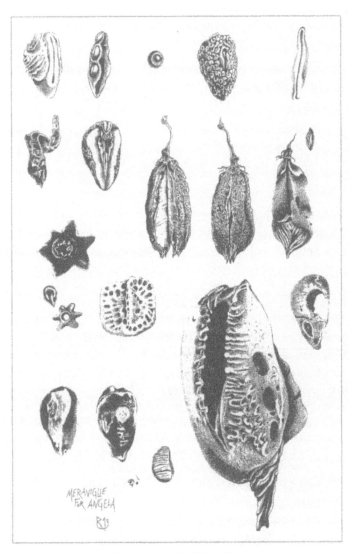

Meraviglie for Angela by Rikki Ducornet

ALPHABETS AND EMPERORS
REFLECTIONS ON KAFKA AND BORGES

Borges was a young man when he translated Kafka, and one imagines that he must have been profoundly haunted. Indeed, the translator, if haunted, is himself a ghost ambulating unseen and unheard in another's *Mundus Imaginalis* which—by the time he is done—has revealed its secrets. The act of translation is of Kabalistic nature: manipulating alphabets—those living bones of language—the object is transcendence: to re-create the luminous complexity of original speech in an alien tongue. The finished work, conjured by a new arrangement of letters, is a vital thing: an old snake in a new skin.

∼

It is Christmas Eve, and very late. The year is 1930, and Borges' translations of Kafka have only just appeared. The moon, Borges' favorite planet, its name *different in different languages and variously lovely (Seven Nights)* is not visible. In the acute darkness, Borges bounds up stairs which are profoundly familiar, yet slams his skull against the cruel edge of an open window. Suspended in delirium, he is for many weeks seized by hallucinatory fevers and incapable of speaking. When, at last, he is able to return to his writing, he sets himself the task to do what he has never done before: to write a piece of "fantastic" fiction. He writes "Pierre Menard, Author of the Quixote"—the story of a man who has so *totally identified* himself with Cervantes and his world, that he is able to produce several chapters of *Don Quixote* which are, in every way, *exactly like the original*. And this is what we ask of a translation: a complicity so entire, and of such potent wizardry, as to lay that living snake at our feet—and its apple—as green as original sin.

I propose that by translating Kafka into Spanish, Borges was himself transformed; that a mysterious operation which combined Kafka, an open window and a moonless night gave us "our" Borges. And that Kafka's story *The Great Wall of China* may be seen as that *small iridescent sphere of almost unbearable brilliance*—the Aleph—in which the future itineraries of Borges' own labyrinths are mirrored.

~

Before I begin my brief if amorous scrutiny of Borges' debt to Kafka, I would like to open two more windows—of glass weirdly fractured—that reveal elements essential to the fictive landscapes of both authors; one window is called Kabala, the other Gnosticism.

The Kabala proposes the peculiar idea that the corporeal universe is that portion of Yahweh's footstool which, thrust from Him and anchored in chaos, emerges from the abysmal waters. Yahweh's configurations—issued from a void he has knowingly created, and which animate His footstool world—are the reflections of dreamed archetypes. All things visible and tangible, from gnats to walruses and carpenters, are but flickerings in the mirror of Yahweh's *whereness*. We enter here into Lands of the Looking Glass; as much as he loved the Kabala and Kafka, Borges loved *Alice*.

Everything happens, Borges writes (in his book titled *Mirrors*), *everything happens and nothing is recorded in these rooms of the looking glass, where magicked into rabbis, we now read the books from right to left.*

Yet, if all the world is semblance, still it is a mirror of sorts, for according to the Kabala, each thing perceived is the fruit, however

the monstrous and the marvelous

volatile, of Divine intention—a shadow of the sublime original. (Which recalls Kafka's complaint that all human language is but a poor *translation*.)

And, in a heretical library of Gnostic books discovered in Fayoum by *fellaheen* looking for bird manure, we read that the visible universe was created by an aborted monster—a hideous chimera with the face of a lion and the body of a snake—which, abandoned by Pistis Sophia—its horrified mother—to a distant corner of the universe where he could not be seen, set about to steal his mother's light. Cementing it with darkness, he created a world—our world.

Both these visions of the planet—submerged footstool and the toy of a bitter demon—admit to the possibility of transcendence. Because the world contains particles of discarded or stolen light, a memory, however faint, of *home*—immaterial and incandescent—nettles the searching mind as a chance of liberation. A possibility invoked by Borges in his short story "The Approach to al-Mu'tasim": *Rethinking the problem (the student) arrives at the mysterious conclusion that "somewhere on the face of the earth is a man from whom this light has emanated; somewhere on the face of the earth there exists a man who is equal to this light." The student decides to spend his life in search of him.*

And echoed in this passage from "The Library of Babel": *Let heaven exist, though my place be in hell. Let me be outraged and annihilated, but for one instant, in one being, let Your enormous library be justified.*

However, in the darkling worlds of both Borges and Kafka, the light is so very dissipated that were we given the Book of Knowledge by Pistis Sophia Herself, we would not find sufficient light to read by. This is Borges' message to us when he describes those library lamps of Babel in the shape of *spherical fruit; the light they emit is insufficient, incessant.* And surely, the most startling metaphor for the spark imprisoned in the cage of corporality is Kafka's portrait of Gregor Samsa waking in the body of a *monstrous vermin*.

For the Gnostic, the body and its hungers are seen as a species of demonic joke; we are, each and every one of us, a Gregor Samsa left to perish in a room cluttered with the archetypes of nightmares, an apple festering in our ribs. Time, Space, and Gravity are the implacable enemies of Spirit; the planet is a malignancy, and the reeling zodiac—the crushing gears and pinions of a mad machine performing without rhyme or reason: *The Penal Colony* on a cosmic scale.

According to the Kabala, Satan rules the world of form and matter —and here the implication is that it is the world's transience which is satanic: the very fact that the world of things is in a continuous state of flux (Abulafia on the Sefer Yezirah).

∾

Now we are ready to investigate *The Great Wall* itself. The wall (and the word, held to a mirror, spells *Law*) is a species of horizontal tower of Babel, and like the tower, an attempt to reach a god who refuses to be reached. Just as in Eden, the god of Babel will not be known, nor named. (In traditional Judaism, YHWH'S name must never be pronounced with its correct vowels; *letters*, which are divine potencies, both activated and participated in the creation of the world. Letters are so potent that a scribe's mistake, as he copies a sacred text, could lead to a cosmic disaster.) The Wall, the confounded Tower and the Forbidden Fruit form a diabolic Trinity: a Trinity of Denial.

The failure of Babel and the loss of a universal language has imposed upon humankind translation as a way of life. Here I cannot help but pause to remember Kafka's account of "sea-sickness" on terra firma—an amnesic state in which the names of things are lost, when *the poplar in the fields which you have named "the tower of Babel" . . . sways again namelessly . . .*

Language, the vehicle of messages and meanings, is central to Kafka's tale. The wall percolates beneath the eye of heaven like a dispatch in Morse code; it is atomized, its syntax riddled with gaps. If, as claims a scholar, the wall is intended as a foundation for a future tower, it is a foundation full of holes: Holy Dogma.

Rumors are everywhere—in the air, on every tongue—as is aborted information. A first messenger is ignored and beaten; his message, written in an archaic dialect, is incomprehensible. A second cannot reach us; between the yawning mouth of a moribund emperor and our own finite ear stretches an infinite[1] obstacle course: *So vast is our land that no fable could do justice to its vastness, the heavens can scarcely span it. . . .*

In other words, the Empire cannot be circumscribed and so cannot be conceived in space; nor can it be mapped and therefore it cannot be found. Unfound, unmapped—can it be said to *exist?* Just as the Emperor's elusive message, the Empire itself is a fiction. The risks of such speculation are so great that the narrator must leave off the telling of his tale, else find himself—a Babel tower of flesh and bone—tumbling from his own faulty foundations: *To set about establishing a fundamental defect here would mean undermining not only our consciences, but, what is worse, our feet.*

The frontiers of such an illusory world, created—as Kafka said to Max Brod *at the instant God looked away*—upon a foundation as porous as lunar cheese, is extended by Borges in his own cruel Babylon. If the destiny of the Emperor of China, sprawling on a shrinking couch,[2] is as tenuous as the wind, and the rumors about him as variable as the weather, *There is nothing so contaminated with fiction as the history of the Company whose orders, issued continuously (perhaps incessantly) do not differ from those lavished by imposters* ("The Lottery of Babylon"). Just as long dead

---

1. For Borges, the idea of an infinite universe is seductive because it contains all virtualities, *including free will.* If infinity is an illusion, then so is freedom. Yet, paradoxically, *the certitude that everything has been written . . . turns us into phantoms* ("The Library of Babel") and dissolves the difference between good and evil ("The Garden of Forking Path").

2. This diminishing Emperor is unintentionally invoked in the *Zohar* where it is a question of God's beard: *The beard is the essence of the whole body, all the splendor of the body follows behind the beard. Thus all is dependent upon the beard* (*The Book of Concealment*).

emperors are set on the throne in Kafka's China, *someone abominably insinuates the Company has not existed for centuries. . . .*

Kafka's China and the Babylon of Borges are, like the window-less and mirror-glazed rooms of a fun house, ruled by willed distortions, cruel illusions, false leads, a *divinity in delirium* ("Library of Babel"); the cosmos *magicked by rabbis* is a hoax. God is a defrauder, Divine Order is reduced to rumor, a game of craps played out by old men in a latrine. It is no accident that in Babylon, there is a sacred latrine name QAPHQA (Kafka). Or that in "The Approach to al-Mu'tasim" (and its subtitle is: *A Game with Shifting Mirrors*) a law student's first step toward transcendence is initiated by the sight of a beggar uri-nating in a disordered garden. Fecal necessity exemplifies the absurd and its incontrovertible determinism: each time we shit we know we are doomed to die. A cognizant vermin, riddled by pride and an enfee-bling awareness of his own finitude and deluded by the capacity to create myths and to succumb to them, man—proconsul, librarian, emperor, or slave—rolls the shit-ball of God's possibility up and down the corridors of a maze of shifting mirrors; in the Library of Babel, *there is a mirror which faithfully duplicates all appearances.*

I always dream of labyrinths or of mirrors, Borges writes (in *Seven Nights*) *. . . the two are not distinct, as it only takes two facing mirrors to construct a labyrinth.*

Yet, even as two facing mirrors offer us an intimation of infinity, and although our spirits reel, we know that we are being deceived; the dung-beetle is being toyed with; what he calls his "perceptions" are a joke.

～

I recall being deeply perturbed when, as a child of ten, I stepped into an elevator in Cairo, the walls of which were made of mirrors; the elevator's vertical function—if real—was finite, and the horizontal capacity—if illusory—was (to use a favorite word of Borges) *inter-minable*. Years later when I took that Borgesian stairway, which *sinks*

the monstrous and the marvelous

abysmally and soars upwards to remote distances, I recognized my vertiginous Egyptian elevator.

But oh, Kitty! says Alice, as she is about to step into the land of Looking-Glass, *Now we come to a passage. You can see a little peep of (it) in Looking-glass House, if you leave the door of our drawing-room wide open: and it's very like our passage as far as you can see, only you know it may be quite different on beyond.*

~

There is a Kabalistic parable in which the mutable world is likened to an infinite set of windows of colored glass which change aspect as the sun passes before them. These windows exemplify the transient aspect of *Mundus Imaginalis*—the unfixed world that is illusion. The sun exemplifies the immutable nature of God.

A number of years ago, I visited the Museum of Science in London and stumbled into a series of darkened rooms in which holograms were on view. The first image I encountered was that of a woman's severed head, which hung suspended in the artificial dusk like the head of an astrological dragon. As I approached, her eyes sparkled with recognition and she flashed me a smile. When at last I could tear myself away from this exemplary encounter, I turned and was greeted by a startling series of spheres about the size of billiard balls. Brightly colored in the classic hues of holography (and, coincidentally, those of a High Priest's breastplate!): carnelian, lapis lazuli, topaz, green jasper—they appeared to spin in deepest space, contained within a phantom grid in an ordered configuration. Because I had been reading Borges at the time—*The library is a sphere whose exact center is any one of its hexagons, and whose circumference is inaccessible*—I played a little game with myself, pretended that I was in the presence of a mockup of the universe, a master plan of divine intention, or—as from some impossible distance—seeing the universe itself, seized in the void and as ordered as an alphabet. For several long minutes I imagined that the cosmos was an alphabet, a set of potencies, seed syllables in the shape of palpitating moons; Borgesian Alephs encompassing all possible worlds simultaneously. But then, shifting my weight from one foot to the other, the spheres dissolved and instantaneously reappeared metamorphosed *into cubes.*

At that moment I recalled Borges' blasphemous sect of librarians which *suggested that the searches* (for the One Book) *should cease and that all men should juggle letters and symbols, until they constructed by chance the Canonical books* ("Library of Babel"). And it seemed to me that the whole Qaphqa–Borgesian problem of the impossibility of ever perceiving the Emperor's new clothes had been offered me in a most unsettling and unforgettable manner. As in that mirrored elevator, I was seized with vertigo.

To end, I offer you the parable of the Emperor's message from *The Great Wall of China* which is about the delusion called Faith and the illusion called God:

> *There is a parable. . . . The Emperor, so it runs, has sent a message to you, the humble subject, the insignificant shadow cowering in the remotest distance before the imperial sun; the Emperor from his deathbed has sent a message to you alone. He has commanded the messenger to kneel down by the bed, and has whispered the message to him; so much store did he lay on it that he ordered the messenger to whisper it back into his ear again. Then by a nod of the head he has confirmed that it is right. Yes, before the assembled spectators of his death — all the obstructing walls have been broken down, and on the spacious and loftily mounting open staircases stand in a ring the great princes of the Empire — before all these he has delivered his message. The messenger immediately sets out on his journey; a powerful, an indefatigable man; now pushing with his right arm, now with his left, he cleaves a way for himself through the throng; if he encounters resistance he points to his breast, where the symbol of the sun*

the monstrous and the marvelous

glitters, the way is made easier for him than it would be for any other man. But the multitudes are so vast, their numbers have no end. If he could reach the open fields how fast he would fly, and soon doubtless you would hear the welcome hammering of his fists on your door. But instead how vainly does he wear out his strength, still he is only making his way through the chambers of the innermost palace; never will he get to the end of them; and if he succeeded in that nothing would be gained; he must next fight his way down the stairs; and if he succeeded in that nothing would be gained; the courts would still have to be crossed; and after the courts the second outer palace; and once more stairs and courts; and once more another palace; and so on for thousands of years; and if at last he should burst through the outermost gate — but never, never can that happen — the imperial capital would lie before him, the center of the world, crammed to bursting with its own sediment. Nobody could fight his way through here even with a message from a dead man. But you sit at your window when evening falls and dream it to yourself.

Stereoscopic Views
Chateaudun. Le Musée and *Jardin d'Acclimatation*

OPTICAL PLEASURE

Who doesn't remember Miss Heart, the tyrant of Fourth Grade, who severely punished Gazing out the Window? Today I wish to inform her ghost—I am certain she is irretrievably dead—that *gazing and dreaming* continue to be what I do most. (As I write this my eye is constantly tempted by the sight of yellow swallowtails gently folding themselves into the orange blossoms of daylilies.)

Boulder-like, Miss Heart cast a Big Shadow. She wore a wig of puddled curls and she had a habit of tugging a hair that sprouted from her chin with unexpected suddenness.

～

Any number of things set off my chronic weakness:

—Edward Lear's paintings of parrots, Man Ray's photograph *Glass Tears*, the glass of Emile Gallé; *Trompe-l'oeil*, the paintings of Vermeer and the etchings of Goya (his *Maya*); lacewings, scarabs, lightning and dragonflies; the ocean, the ceramic dishes of Bernard Palissy. (In the second half of the sixteenth century, Palissy made casts of snakes, lizards, frogs, and other small creatures: snails, eels, crayfish—and also leaves and seaweed and vines. These he used to decorate dishes glazed in natural colors; little mirrors of the world, they seem to quicken with life. So generously do they nourish the eye that a minute's look quiets the soul for hours.)

—Paradises, true and false: the Tea Palace in Mantova is a prime example with its sham grotto and alchemical ceiling painted by Giulio Romano. Romano designed the palace for the Duke Federico Gonzaga in the early sixteenth century, and despite the ravages of time and the fact that the palace is no longer isolated from the rest of the world by water, it remains one of the most enchanting places in the world. Its rooms—ceilings and walls—throng with the creatures of Romano's flamboyant imagination: grotesques sporting extravagant erections, eroticized fishermen (clearly the inspiration behind some of Salvador Dali's paintings), divine lovers, battling centaurs, an entire room in trick perspective devoted to giants with a mosaic floor in the shape of a vortex, alchemical conundrums and a vestibule ceiling painted with a trellis of grapes circled by tigers, cupids, and goats. (And what a delight it was this past November to stumble upon a large erotic painting of Romano's in the Hermitage, after being assaulted by an infinity of crucifixions!)

—The serpents painted by Jacopo Ligozzi, anything painted by Bosch or Maria-Sybilla Merian; greenhouses, most fountains, the bronze centaurs I once saw at a flea market and neglected to buy, nineteenth-century stereoviews of Celan. My infant son in the instants after his birth afforded me such acute optical pleasure I thought I might perish with delight; the memory of Uma Thurman's face at the age of nine; anything painted by Max Ernst or conceived by Joseph Cornell; Breugel's *Tower of Babel*, Tenniel's illustrations for *Alice*.

—A mural painted by Max Ernst for Paul Eluard's house called *Au premier mot limpide*. Rosamond Purcell's photographs and in particular her picture of the wax portrait of an Italian albino from the Renaissance (which is also the portrait of twins with black wings I once encountered in a dream).[1]

—Turmeric. Anthropomorphic landscapes. Just about any paint-

---

1. They appear in a short story called "The Neurosis of Containment," in *The Word Desire* (Henry Holt 1997).

the monstrous and the marvelous

ing showing Saint Francis being tempted by the devil. Lions, tigers, the books of Jurgis Baltrušaitis. Phosphenes. The unexpected sight of a rattlesnake sunning in the path, or, as in the Yucatan, a large black tarantula crossing the road. The false eyes on the wings of butterflies. Suddenly I recall a room in a museum of Natural History in Angers, France: an oval room filled with the bodies of white birds.

—Palenque.

—The entire bestiary of Aloys Zötl, who never once saw in the flesh the creatures he painted.

—*Capricorn beetles. The spots on their backs vary tremendously and make up a species of alphabet or code: two finger-tip spots, one robber's mask, two coins; two finger-tip spots, one robber's mask with horns, two coins; two finger-tip spots joined to a kite, a bat wing, two coins; sometimes there are four coins and sometimes no coins and instead two diamonds, or a disc, or a disc like a flying saucer, its landing-gear unfolded (The Cult of Seizure).*

—I have never seen a piece of glass by Dale Chihuly that did not cause me delight. Imagine fire, sea foam and weather—including thunderstorms—congealed to potencies, or the impossible artifacts of dreams surging into the real, and you may begin to have an inkling of the beauty and mystery of this master's glass. Even his simple cylinders appear to belong to another planet, and his bowls could be the grails of some freer universe. Once, when walking in downtown Toronto, I saw a fire just ahead of me, a fantastic play of color and light. It turned out to be an exhibit of Chihuly's glass, set out on glass tables illumed from beneath, and perceived through the large glass windows of the gallery.

—The original edition of the *Encyclopaedia Britannica* of 1768– 1771 of which I own a replica. Plate LXXIV (Book Two) contains the following:

1. an Electrical Machine
2. a Cloud Machine
3. an Elephant

4. an Echeneis
5. an Elater
6. an Erinaceus or Hedge Hog
7 & 8. Ermin and Ermine (Heraldric Crests)

—Those mysterious blue pages! When I was a girl, friends of my parents brought me a large number of gray pages covered with mysterious pale blue photographs, not much larger than stamps, of Renaissance paintings, ancient artifacts from Greece, Rome, and the Middle East. There were floor plans of places for the most part impossible to identify, Florentine capitols, even peculiar looking tableware, such as extravagant soup tureens. I can still feel the aesthetic charge of those curious pages , and long with all my heart to see them again. But they are as intangible as the pages from a book of dreams.

∾

There is a marvelous short story by the Brazilian writer Clarice Lispector; its subject is Optical Pleasure. It is called *The Imitation of the Rose*. Like Angela Carter's *A Company of Wolves*[2] and José Donoso's *The Walk*, it is a most disquieting *and* deeply satisfying tale of domestic subversion—except that it is far darker than the other two, whose heroines evolve toward radical affirmations of being. Lispector's Laura, on the other hand, allows herself two impossible choices only: to embrace nonidentity, or to flee the seductions of Beauty by taking a fast train to Mars (psychotic break). At the end she opts for Mars; traveling at the speed of light she disrupts all established chronologies.

Laura's eyes are brown; *as for green eyes, it seemed to her that if she had green eyes it would be as if she had not told her husband everything.* In fact, like her brown dress, her brown eyes are a disguise. Greenness circulates

---

2. Come to think of it, Angela introduced me to Lispector's work around the time that *A Company of Wolves* was being made into a movie.

the monstrous and the marvelous

inside them, just as red circulates inside the dangerous white roses she dares not keep for herself. Laura looks at the roses *in rapture . . . like someone depraved*. Just as Carter's wolves *fatten on darkness*, so Laura wolves the roses down with eyes greener and greener. Their beauty's claim upon her is entire and irreversible. Already impossibly remote at the end of the story, she is seized by speed. Optical Pleasure snapping at her heels, Beauty beckoning her on, Beauty nowhere near her. If eyes feed on light, Laura's eyes, burning far too brightly, have solarized her. Lispector characterizes her luminosity as *shamelessness*.

~

If you burn their stems, poppies hold themselves together long enough to be painted. The poppy has its own fauna — black bugs not much bigger than grains of pepper. When the bugs are not climbing up and down the furry ladders of the stems, they sit on the petals facing the sun like seedlings (The Cult of Seizure).

~

Yesterday Clarissa Pinkola Estes came for lunch and asked me if the melon that was poised in the center of the table *had an eye*. I told her that the day before while I was taking a nap, I heard the call of a bird which, in my mind's eye, caused *a hole in the sky*, or *in the skin of the day*. I asked her if an experience of this nature was what she meant, and as it turned out, it was. After her departure, I picked up G. Cabrera Infante's book on Ramón Alejandro, ¡*Vaja Papaya!* and found myself gazing into a sea of eyes contained within the halved body of a papaya or "Castillian melon." G. Cabrera Infante notes that in Cuba the papaya is called *la fruta bomba* and that in Yoruba the word *embomba* designates the vulva. Ramón's Afro-Cuban paintings are filled with the seeds of allegorical and necromantic fruits that gaze out at the viewer seductively, and with a certain insolence.

Grand Theaters of tropical nature, in the tradition of the lush landscapes of Johann Moritz Rugendas and Karl Friedrich Philipp von Martius, or the sumptuous arrangements of Brazilian fruits by Albert Eckhout or Frans Jans, Ramón's paintings abound in the fruits of Cuba, not only papayas, but also pineapples, star and custard apples, guavas, guanabanas, tamarinds, bananas, okras, mangoes, alligator pears, coconuts. . . . These "theaters" radiate light, illumed not so much by Olorun's sky—which is often overcast if not downright stormy—but by these seeded bodies, split apart, molten and bright as lanterns.

Theaters of Divination also, the stage may be strewn with magic dice, feathers, mirrors, candles, coins and cards, and cones of potent stones crowned with spirit catchers; they are sometimes guarded by death-smelling, ghost-seeing and lascivious dogs, or jackal-headed Anubis himself, or animated by archangels. Or the fruits are transformed into death makers stuck with nails and knotted with strips of colored cloth; they are presented on altars or within cages perhaps to capture useful spirits. These structures acquire extreme and baroque forms recalling the anthropomorphic cabinets and table clocks of the Renaissance; some evoke savage machines of possession: Erzsébet Bathory's iron maiden; Sadean furniture. But for the most part, Ramón's *Anima Mundi* are wonderfully erotic, even whimsical, recalling the unique arrangements Bower Birds display for the delectation of potential mates in their own theaters of seduction.

∾

Lewis Carroll took pictures from 1856 to 1880. Among these are a portrait of a medical student and amateur photographer Carroll admired, posed standing beside a human skeleton and that of a small ape. Leaning on a staff and reaching out as if to grasp the human hand of bone, the ape seems to be beseeching its counterpart to pay attention to the startling similarity that exists between them.[3] A second photograph taken the same year offers up an emu reduced to bone. Standing on a little table (very like the one Tenniel drew for *Alice in Wonderland* flourishing a key and a bottle of DRINK ME) the emu leans into the void above a label inscribed with its name.

Both photographs raise the haunting problem of identity, a recurrent theme in the *Alice* books. Bones of apes and men, juxtaposed, question the Son of Adam's divine origin, just as Alice's tumble into Wonderland has her asking: *Who in the world am I? Ah, that's the great puzzle!* And like Humpty Dumpty in Looking Glass land, the emu has a name, but has lost its sense. (If its name *is* Apterix australis, it is only *called* emu.)

Carroll's dream: *Alice's Adventures in Wonderland and Through the Looking Glass*, and Tenniel's illuminations of that dream are among the world's chief delights. But then, so are Carroll's photographs—and he was one of the world's first great portrait photographers—above all, his pictures of little girls. If everyone knows how much Carroll loved little girls, not everyone knows that he loved them so much he signed his first published poems *Louisa Carolina*. Perhaps, as is my conviction, he *was* a little girl disguised by fate as a cautious don with a sweet, sad face and flyaway hair—a stutterer, deaf in one ear, who idolized Euclid and talked to himself. As does Alice: *I'm sure I'm not Ada ... for her hair goes in such long ringlets, and mine doesn't go in ringlets at all; and I'm sure I can't be Mabel, for I know all sorts of things, and she, oh, she knows such a very little! Besides, she's she, and I'm I, and—oh dear, how puzzling it all is!*

Lewis Carroll's respectful tenderness for his "Amelias"—a favorite name of his—is matched only by his ferocious nonsense that delights in unmasking human folly in its most troublesome form— irrational and abusive authority. The creatures of Wonderland do their very best to bully Alice and frighten her, but she always confronts

---

3. Morton N. Cohen in *Lewis Carroll: A Biography* notes that "the photograph, taken in 1857, predates the controversy engendered by the publication of Darwin's *On the Origin of Species by Natural Selection* by two years."

tyranny with common sense and self-possession. This fearlessness—
Who cares for you? You're nothing but a pack of cards!"—is tangible in
Carroll's portraits of the "real" Alice who was, in Carroll's words: *An
entirely fascinating seven year old maiden.* May those who persist in thinking
Carroll was a covert pederast look with open eyes at his pictures of
Alice Liddell which invariably reveal not only the photographer's
admiration for his model but her calm beneath his gaze, the active
intelligence with which she poses. In fact, all Carroll's dream girls are
dreamy, intent and unafraid; not one among them fidgets or looks
askance. Such is Carroll's genius, each portrait conveys the integrity
of personality that exemplifies a healthy child; in other words: *selfhood.*

Alice was a gorgeous child and in Carroll's company, clearly as
free as the wind (even if, to be photographed, she had to sit *very* still
for forty-five seconds). *We were absolutely fearless with him,* another of his
favorites, Dymphna Ellis, recalled in later years. . . . *I never catch a whiff
of the potent odour of collodion,* a mature Alice would herself recall, *without
instantly being transported on the magic wings of memory to Lewis Carroll's dark
room. . . . He was indeed a bringer of delight in those dim, far-off days.*

In Carroll's most famous picture of her, her unforgettable face
framed by the soft shadow of her hair, Alice Liddell stands in rags,
spritely and undauntable, the portrait of childhood in all its promise
(and, it must be said, the mirror opposite of a portrait Carroll took of her
married and seemingly sunk with despondency into a very ugly chair).
Even in finery the child Alice is like a sunbeam seized only to dissolve.
All the fleetingness of childhood is here and more: Alice not only radi-
ates light, she personifies it. Elsewhere in profile she appears to navigate
the day; in her able hand the back of her chair is like the tiller of a boat.
This pilot could dissolve a turtle-soup fog with the intensity of her stare.

Lewis Carroll was born Charles Lutwidge Dodgson in a place
named Daresbury. It seems that Daresbury is the place where these
pictures were taken. He called them: "dreams," "moments," "beauty"; he
called them: "memory."

HAUNTING BY WATER

My father had a beautiful library, now lost. Among books once exquisitely tangible was a turquoise volume that contained a photograph of two Mexican youths standing naked and navel-deep in water. They faced the camera's cyclopean eye solemnly, even grimly—as though the act of image-making were fraught with danger, and water the element of anguish, not pleasure.

The photographer and his models had been standing upon uneven ground, so that the entire scene was off-kilter, veering dangerously to the right: the Pacific was kept from sliding over the world's edge by the page's neutral frame.

The word for sea in Latin, *mare*, is derived from the word for desert, and the picture in the book—so pale it might have been taken in dense fog—gave me my first acute impression of absence. I was just old enough to recognize that if the camera had fixed the image of the two living boys much as dead hair is fixed within a locket, then they had escaped vanishment only momentarily. Suspended in limbo, those grim faces and that desolate sea conveyed this message: time is dissolution, space an illusion—and both exemplify loss.

This revelation is photography's illuminating paradox: what we see is an instant in time which, like certain deep-water starfish, dissolves the instant it is seized. Photography exhibits are inevitably eerie and engender melancholy; nothing conveys the world's instability and our own transience better. (A painting evolves in time and so its process is always more or less tangible; because it can never be "real" in the way a photograph is "real," a painting rarely produces as acute a sense of *dislocation*.)

Which brings us to the painter-photographer David Hockney and his series of paintings of pools—many of which appear to have been painted after photographs, although, it seems to me that Hockney's eye is almost invariably a glass eye. The work—highly colored, decorative (Hockney also paints for the stage), often whimsical in the manner of Saul Steinberg (but Hockney is never *as* whimsical, nor, I think, as brilliant as Steinberg), dramatic, even droll— is suspended, disengaged. The paintings are as smooth as the skin of a pool on a windless morning. Here stillness is absence, the world a limbo-land, a sickle-sharp parenthesis; the pool as existential anteroom, exile. The figures in this series—swimming, standing, *floating*—all appear spiritually swamped. *Peter* (1964) is as inscrutable as a rubber duck; *Portrait of Nick Wilder* (1966) offers another rubber toy figure, bobbing before a cartoon villa. The overall effect is reminiscent of Steinberg's scathing California sketches, revelatory glimpses of the American way of being vain.

Other pools are painted with comical calligraphy as though the water represented a cat's cradle. Graphically playful, their mood is ominous—the water's knotted script snaking about the swimmers' truncated bodies, netting them in.

Presented like photographic slides, *The Splash* (1966) and *A Bigger Splash* (1967) offer images of water in the instants after a dive and in which the diver, swallowed whole, is not visible. Both convey not only loss but silence—the soundless climax of a distant star. The sky and landscapes beyond are emblematic, and the structures—those spare houses of the rich—as enigmatic as the walls of de Chirico's phantom cities.

With no figures to disturb the geometric and pictographic rigor of inner tube, glazed tile, towel, guard rail, inflated mattress, and rubber ball, *Four Different Kinds of Water* (1967) proposes a world reduced to ciphers, potent elements (but also ambiguous and unreliable) in the game of revelation; a set of koans, elegant and severe. My favorite in the series is a gorgeous study in crayon (*Study of Water, Phoenix, Arizona, 1976*), a glimpse of transience as seduction. Indigo, pale green, reflected orange, turquoise—this water *moves*, is truly water, not its sign, and the play of shadow and light, of deep and shallow places—is hot and engaging. This water recalls the Aztec's conviction that the gods themselves were born of water, and the Mexican baptismal formula: *All of us are children of Chalchihuitlycue, Goddess of Water*. This pool promises something like delight.

Photo by Jonathan Cohen

MAPPING PARIS

One late afternoon of early winter in the hour when the skies and streets of Paris take on the color of turtledoves, I stumbled into a dead end that angled curiously backward like a broken finger, and found myself gazing into the window of a shop unlike any other I had ever seen, for it contained a dazzling assortment of anamorphoses, some several hundred years old. The anamorphosis, like Nabokov's *nonnons*, needs to be reflected on the curved surface of a conic or tubular mirror in order to be seen. The painted image, often wildly erotic, scatologic or anticlerical, is purposely distorted and, without its mirror, incomprehensible. The shop window in Paris offered both the anamorphoses and their looking-glasses—a bewitching sight, a species of witchcraft by a picture. At the time, I was too poor to buy one although I would have gladly sold my soul for one, and body too, but the proprietor, decrepit and cranky was nonplussed and I, having glutted my eyes on scatological and satirical scenes, peeled off into the street with the promise I would return the following spring. But this was Paris, and by then the shop had vanished beneath the sand of minutes and hours. The broken finger had twisted itself into a goose neck, the impasse had vanished from both maps and the minds of men, and no one I questioned in the quarter had ever heard the word "anamorphosis." They treated me like an escapee from Le Collège Pataphysique. I wandered about sadly, following my nose past the red horses' heads of Butchers', a shop full of glass eyes, glass marbles, mother-of-pearl brooches and buttons and, strangely, hard candy. I passed a window animated by artificial and articulated limbs, and a minuscule establishment offering bricks of chocolate so black the sidewalk was suddenly submerged in shadow. The anamorphoses were gone forever, but later that day on Rue de Seine I found a book devoted to Mandrakes and so returned to my hotel soothed, if nevertheless needled by thoughts of mutability and thwarted desire.

In another year and another season, leaving the gâre d'Austerlitz behind me and crossing over to the Natural History Museum, I heard laughter and, stepping into a pocket-sized garden, saw a puppeteer lift her skirts to reveal a face painted on her belly; her navel made for a very droll mouth and her pubis a very merry beard, indeed. A vendor of ices pedaled past on a *triporteur* painted purple; the ices he sold were flavored with violets, a flavor which that day matched the color of the sky, exactly, and the eyes of the Siamese twins, Helen and Philomène, who are forever suspended in a jar in the museum's chamber of comparative anatomy.

$\sim$

Paris cannot be contained. A mammoth *nonnon* or anamorphosis —erotic, political, anticlerical and surreal—it is as mutable as Isis, the city's own *anima*, and as eternal. If Paris could be pinned down, she would gather herself up on all her one hundred legs in an instant and scramble off in new shoes, leaving a smell of Turkish tobacco behind her. If Paris could be bottled she would taste something like Pernod, a salt tear, a smoked mackerel, a drop of blood, the crushed petals of azaleas, the skin of a new lover, the marrow of roast duckling, champagne sorbet, the damp of moonless nights, couscous, a heap of freshly laundered old lace, a fur muff, autumn leaves, axle grease, a fine old bottle of ink, Norman butter, and eels cooked with prunes.

the monstrous and the marvelous

Paris is all those people who look at you while you are licking her windows and drinking her in. Those people you look at too, who like Touaregs inhabit the air and navigate shafts of light. The unknown stranger who in a dream inspires untold longing is, *sans doute*, someone you saw in Paris bent over an *express*, or a book, or gazing into the heart of a flower at Le Jardin Botanique. The acute melancholy you feel when a piece of cheese nibbled in Manhattan turns out to be sublime is only Paris uncoiling and resurging in your breast. And when in San Francisco you buy a pair of shoes so green they can never be worn, it is because they brought to mind a pair you saw on Rue de Grenelle exhibited among orchids in an artificial rain.

All this to say: Paris cannot be mapped. (Only Joseph Cornell came close with his star charts and boxes of shifting sand.) To navigate Paris successfully, one needs to be something of a Touareg, something of a daredevil, and something of a deep sea diver. In other words, one needs to be something of a chimera or enigma oneself, a mythical creature ready for and worthy of Wonderland. Such a one has revealed herself in the mutable shape of Karen Elizabeth Gordon, who has in between fits of mad laughter come up with lyrical itineraries based on those hazards that track and impel travelers worth their salt in the city of dreams. For example, in *Paris Out of Hand*, a guide unlike any other, and one we have never quite managed to do without, she directs us to the *Hotel des Horloges* where time is the handmaiden of disposition, the *Hotel Carrington* where you will be registered by a debutante disguised as a hyena (although, watch out! It could be the other way 'round); the *Hotel Quadrille*, a favorite haunt of perambulating lobsters, and the *Petit Hôtel du Moyen-Age*, where a pair of ermine slippers awaits you. You won't want to miss *Brasserie Loplop*, *Le Cadavre Exquis* and *Café Nada* — *malgré les piéges surrealistes*; and should you be a dog, *Patte à la Main* proposes barking biscuits. *Café Conjugal* is a must for couples atomizing as well as on the mend, but the place I long for is *Café Frangipane*: I want to order the *Lalique* despite the price, and also the *Tonique*, which *delivers a wallop of well-being*. Other offerings include *Le Metro Marquis de Sade, le Grand Magasin Molière, the Counterfeit Museum* and *Arse Poetica* where you can buy fur pants and butt art; *le Grenier de Tante Amélie* where anything and everything you have ever lost — tonsils, lovers, teeth — may be found; *la Toucherie* where, if you are charming enough, you get to see the plum's secret underside before you have to pay for it.

THE MONSTROUS AND THE MARVELOUS

It is a poor reverie which invites a nap.
— Gaston Bachelard

Perhaps it could be argued that the Monstrous and the Marvelous are all that give both the things of the world, and our capacity to receive them, their original keenness, their primary fire. A monster, preserved at birth in a jar of thick glass and glowing in the fading sunlight of a museum, is all at once infused with poetry, just as a pebble taken up from the path, whose embedded fossil offers the image of an eye, takes on magical intensity. One cannot toss such a thing away. I once owned a thin slice of marble, which, on its polished surface showed a violent seascape, including a grotto awash with foam and animated by sea birds, a crashing surf, and, beyond, a raging ocean. This accidental image was like the gift of the sea itself and more: it offered a potent first seeing each time I gazed at it. Such moments disrupt habits of thought and subvert the general devitalization of contemporary life — its baneful impostors and impositions.

When Anton van Leeuwenhoek was startled by the sight of *little animals* living in a drop of rain, he was given an instant in Eden: he enjoyed the first quality of sight. The creatures were unlike anything anyone had ever seen. He called them *the most wretched imaginable.* They lived in a tangle, had horns and unbearably thin feet, and tails *coiled up serpent-wise after the fashion of copper or iron wire that, having been wound close about a round stick, and then taken off, kept all its windings.* When some of these little creatures were put in a dry place, having *lain moving their little feet for a while, they burst asunder . . . imagine, for example,* Leeuwenhoek continues, *that you have a sheep's bladder filled with shot, peas, and water; then, if you were to dash it apieces on the ground, the shot, peas, and water would scatter themselves all over the place.*

This curious analogy seems unintentionally whimsical, but its vividness reveals Leeuwenhoek's visual excitement, an excitement that clearly stimulated his imagination. And it brings to mind the monstrous fabulations of the marvelous literary madmen of France, such as Delhommeau the Elder, who one day *having nothing better to do* looked very closely at a ball. After much reflection and motivated by some obscure instinct, he came to the conclusion that the ball contained a major mystery. He baptized it "Mysterious Ball," and wrote a fourteen-page pamphlet about it. In other words, sometimes one need merely look at a thing long enough to see how marvelous and how monstrous—and mysterious—it is.

1. Last Things First

> *Last things first and the itching contusion*
> *of accident (after chance rolled thru) . . .*
> (—Ann Lauterbach, from "Night Barrier")

Harry Mathews'[1] marvelous reveries always evoke the dangers and potencies inherent in randomness and the inexhaustible pleasures of chance. The many forms his reveries take: journals, novels, "preverbs," "snips of the tongue," stories and poems, engage a geometry of longing, longing lovingly pursued in secret and arcane variations: playful, philosophical, unashamedly human; wistful, too.

---

1. Harry Mathews is the only American member of Oulipo (le Ouvroir de Littérature Potentielle), a Paris-based group of writers and mathematicians, founded in 1961 by Raymond Queneau and François le Lionnais.

the monstrous and the marvelous

Harry is the inventor of Mathews' algorithm, a literary machine that can, in his words, *juggle not only episodes of fiction . . . but entire books, indeed entire literatures and civilizations, planets, solar systems, galaxies. . . .* The algorithm and other subtle self-perpetuating machines—most of them as transparent as air (less machines than pliant maps, perhaps, with shifting boundaries and mutable weather, impressable, percolating and revelatory)—are the energies behind worlds which in the words of his vanished friend Georges Perec are *loaded with resonance.*

Mathews' algorithm, which reduces the library of Babel and the lottery of Babylon to an equation the size of a postage stamp, is only one of an infinite number of monstrous innovations, acute subversions, marvelous hoaxes and mournful delights. Among these:

> a plague vaccine delivered by wasps,
> an orgasmic dental drill,
> the undetectable racing horse fix,
> the minute, measuring doglet, Limnisse,
> a male dancer netted and dipped in strong glue,
> an entire French village swept up and away by a dizzying
>   recipe for roast lamb (Mathews' fictions abound in
>   ceremonial duties that are transformed to vortices, or
>   that evoke the crises of existence),
> a sacred ritual in which a Queen rubs down her King with
>   gum and seven hundred seeds,
> a game in which emblematic worms spelling their way
>   across a damp table end the race (as it always ends and
>   for all of us: badly) in the ponderous claws of crabs.

If chance encounters set Mathews' gears in motion, his fictional words are self-reflecting and self-perpetuating: they always reveal something about the nature of chance and of chaos, too: *At the risk of betraying my goal of including everything, I concentrate my descriptions of events. It's their rhythm that's hard to catch (The Journalist).*

2. Mutable as Embers

Lurid, haphazard,
decorated with dew, a dossier
begins to fill. Gates
form, and the migratory shapes, mutable as embers.
Under the logo of a furnace the collections spread.
     (—Ann Lauterbach, from "Poem of the Landscape")

In *Le Miroir du Merveilleux* Pierre Mabille writes: *Every individual is a reflecting surface, small or big, straight or oblique, tarnished or brilliant, by which the universe is reflected transformed.*

Rosamond Wolff Purcell was born with a third eye. If this eye is luminous, it is also very heavy: an extra allowance of gravity. But Rosamond was also born with wings, and to watch her in action is to spy upon an angel informed by ether, fallen from a lighter world.

She is something of a phantom, too, haunting those secret cabinets where obsessively accumulated collections have slept for decades scored in dust. She loves this dust almost as much as the object it nets: *curiosities* suspended in their glass bells sparked with bubbles of air.

Of her camera, Rosamond says: *there are no tricks in the box, it captures what is there.*

When Rosamond Purcell takes pictures in the waning light in a lost room of a Dutch museum, the result is of such sweet lucency the images look as if they had been taken through a lens of amber. We are in Wonderland; the March Hare is always very near. And the Red Queen: many of these bottled beasts are now extinct, sent over the edge by the same men who would attempt to stop time with the taxidermist's poison pins.

Everything the photographer seizes has both light and gravity. She has metamorphosed the world into emblems: moth wing, fetal monkey, skeletons and skins are all reduced to precious signs, powers and planets. These creatures posing in their glass houses are gods and masters: Eden belongs to them.

Of the collection jars, Rosamond says: *When you place one in the light it opens up into rooms. It extends outward.*

By "systematizing" junk of all kinds—antique bars of soap, fractured machines, bones, beaks, books devoured by worms or fire or made into nests by rats, toys rusted nearly to oblivion, partially digested pins—Rosamond also creates bogus collections, marvelous museums of the mind. Disrupting the closed systems of public or private collections (of *naturalia*—including anomalies—and *artificialia*) and reorganizing them, she elaborates novel ways of ordering, articulating and dreaming the world.

Recently, I asked her about one of her more troubling pictures, a slice of a hydrocephalic infant's face. What remains of that face in the jar, she told me, reminds her of many things: the masked ball described in Alain Fournier's *Le Grand Meaulnes*, Henri Rousseau's painting of the masked harlequin, the face of the moon in Melies' movie *Voyage dans la Lune*, and Edgar Allan Poe's *The Masque of the Red Death*.

Of her work she says: *I have my reasons.*

If Purcell authenticates her artifacts by offering them in formal sequences that appear to include "variants" of a prime topic, it is in much the same way as Ben Marcus, in his *Age of Wire and String*, subverts and reinvents the language of tracts, manuals and monographs, they accumulate "proof" until the truth of the dream is established unequivocally.

Marcus' project is visionary in the best sense and evokes the Surrealist enterprise—the great collage novels of Max Ernst, for example, but also the satiric drawings of J. J. Grandville, so essential to Ernst's vision and occasionally (and, I imagine, coincidentally) a mirror of Marcus' own. In an age *looted of secrets*, a faulty age barely held together with wire and string, Ben Marcus sets about to renew vision and reinstate mystery.

In this flawed and treacherous age, fornicating with the corpse of the resuscitated wife animates the toaster and vacuum cleaner;

decoders sit on the beds of dreamers deciphering desperate messages scrambled by snores. The air supply depends upon superstitious fasting, and sleepers perform specific functions such as warding off birds or enabling those awake to copulate, eat, and speak. Speech, however, is often lethal: the son may be eaten alive by the father's words. Inevitably eaten by the gnostical father, a son is first and foremost food. And if fathers devour their sons, they also smash houses, and smash in the teeth of the son who dares *begin his prayer in the middle*.

Clothes make the man; we are what we eat. Such platitudes are awarded new and unsettling life. Among other marvels, Marcus proposes a brother built from food and the *food costumes of Montana*, woven of noodles and worn with taffy ankle bindings and a fudge girdle.

To return to Purcell, if you are fortunate enough to visit her imaginary collections, you will see a proliferation of astonishingly beautiful photographs:

> the skull of a pirate and a suicide,
> the wax portrait of an albino Apollo with eyes of palest pink,
> the mouth and nose of a Spaniard in a bottle,
> a book metamorphosed by the passage of time into the seed pod of a Natural History conceived in fever, or sets of carved dentures transmuted to the fossil records of an extinct species of worms.

This last photograph could also be a page in a book borrowed from Mathews' imagined library of the Earls of Mar, entitled *The Natural History of the Human Teeth*. And I would not be surprised to see *an armchair made of wax . . . indented in every part by the marks of human teeth that had bitten hard into its surface (The Conversions)* materialize in Purcell's uncharted regions, alongside Marcus' inventions from *The Age of Wire and String*:

universal storm calendar
alloy of water
shirt of noise
atmospheric food and the
    musical testimony of insects

3. The Talisman

Dip the talisman in rain.
Where, what message?
            (—Ann Lauterbach, from "The Return of Weather")

Randall Heath[2] is the maker of lovingly crafted peep shows. His process is similar to a hurricane's: he lifts things from their moorings and sets them down again in eerie and elaborate configurations.

Randall constructs prim looking boxes of white pine fitted with a hole. Self-animating kaleidoscopes, these are equipped with motors and lights and evoke Mathews' wheelworks as much as the marvelous reliquaries of some other age "of wire and string." Above all they quicken the senses and propose the *original qualities* of things (to borrow from Bachelard). Artificial leaves and flowers, old photographs, glass bottles filled with red water and throbbing with longing, the face of a man who may be howling with laughter or pain; glass berries and memory forests, figures puzzled together—all these offer glimpses of the world just after the fall. An eye to the peephole, one is startled by the unexpected play of light, the mutable tricks of mirrors. Time in the shapes memory takes has ennobled trash and transmuted it to potencies.

Here is a partial description of Randall's experience of a cemetery in Prague which offers a window into his work:

---

2. Randall Heath is an artist and graphic designer, and a founding editor of *Rain Taxi Review of Books*.

The compartments themselves were a fairly shallow space, compact, yet deep enough to contain an array of objects. Foremost was the urn, the physical remains reduced to ash and bits of tiny fragmented bone. The urns seemed to vary in size and preciousness — according to the degree of wealth the owner possessed — but were mostly monolithic vases embellished with gold lettering perfunctorily recording name, date of birth, and demise. Suddenly I was reminded of the time when as a child I was taken to the cemetery of old Philadelphia. As we wandered around the grounds my mind was set spinning by the cracked and crumbling graves, for I was sure that I could see within a jumble of bones and dust. And it was as if I were given a window and was seeing into the past, a simultaneous past which existed there alongside my own. There impressed upon the child's mind was the secret mystery of time. Or rather simply, the evidence of time. And so in Prague it all came flooding back, or was it simply a recollection of a state of mind?

4. The Book of Hanging Gardens

on each cusp a dove
on each palm a grove (love)
        (—Ann Lauterbach, from "A clown, Some Colors . . .")

G. Cabrera Infante evokes Arcimboldo when he moons over the paintings of Ramón Alejandro,[3] voluptuous paintings in which the fruits of Eden offer sexual and magical powers to the gorging eye. They also evoke the painter's friend Severo Sarduy; Severo's vision of a Caribbeanized transvestite (infinitely transforming and desirable) cosmos. The universe is here the lyrical theater of Desire; the shape of time determined not by endings but by those rituals of the famished mind which assume eternal hunger. Feast your eyes.

---

3. Ramón Alejandro is a Cuban painter living in Miami. His paintings are further described in "Optical Pleasure."

5. Shards of Found Delight

> *Shards of found delight*
>> (—Ann Lauterbach, from "Poem of the Landscape")

Perec once described what he called the *narratème*, a *tiny element . . . like a pearl . . . which will gradually become fiction, become the narration.* When I was a small child, I was "stung" by an illustration of a bee whenever I opened a particularly beloved book. And the corpse of a red fox swarming with a multitude of bees has always been my cipher for transmutation, my *narratème*, the black pearl, the *zahir* of my own imagining mind. In the safety of a child's room flooded with sunlight, a painted bee will forever have the power to sting, and in a summer's wood, a humming corpse to embrace beauty. For me, to be is "to bee" or "to be beed." To be stung into a reverie of acute wakefulness and watchfulness; to be struck alive with wonder.

Wonderment and horror reverberate throughout the mind, the one with lucency and the other in shadow, an incapacitating opacity, perhaps: what David Matlin[4] calls "traumatic obscurity" and "toxic consequence." There is a paradox here worthy of our attention: if the marvelous may be informed and animated by the monstrous, the monstrous leaves the marvelous no air, no light, no room. Yet Matlin's experience teaching poetry to men in Hell demonstrates the truth of Bachelard's conviction that *Poetry is one of the destinies of speech.*

6. "A Dreamland Never Described"

Mysterious, humorous and disquieting, Can Xue's stories[5] conjure Kafka, not only because of the limpidity of her style which is bone-clean and lyrical, but because of the weirdly tragic yet exem-

---

4. I am referring to David Matlin's *Vernooykill Creek: The Crisis of Prisons in America* (San Diego State University Press, 1997).

5. See Can Xue's *The Embroidered Shoes* (New York: Henry Holt, 1997).

plary lives of her characters. The faceless, languid, "mimosa child" in "The Child Who Raised Poisonous Snakes" does strange things even *without going outdoors*. He has the extraordinary capacity to see and be bitten by, to bite and to capture the "flowery" snakes of his imagination. Like thoughts looking for a mind, or dreams in search of a dreamer, the child gathers up the lonely snakes of his solitude. These haunt his parent's house like hungry ghosts.

But if this odd child is the keeper of snakes, he is also responsible for their destruction, and in a wildly inventive shift of plot, the parents—who have somehow managed to make the child the martyred instrument of their own terror—become, *with the child's help*, literal dream-slaughterers, the killers of the flowery snakes. This accelerates their descent into death.

For the sake of apparent harmony, the dream snakes drop from the child's mind into his belly. But if they are more deeply hidden, still the child continues to raise them—his quiet way of raising hell. Keeping snakes he has become the guardian of his parent's mortality. If once the snakes exemplified the most dangerous thoughts of the imagining mind, curiosity and the will to wander, they now exemplify the unstoppable passage of time. Unable to acquire autonomy, the faceless child can only dream of death and finally, become death's keeper. His predicament is much like Gregor Samsa's, but if Samsa's parents glut on their son's disfigurement and death, the faceless child's deteriorate: *They were simply worn out.*

In "A Dreamland Never Described," the Recorder of dreams, sitting in his shack by the roadside, *having abandoned everything*, informs our memory of Kafka's Hunger Artist whose own acutely rigorous professional ethics are of no interest to anyone and who over time dwindles away. Like the Hunger Artist, the Recorder does what he does not from choice, inclination or even talent, but because he cannot help himself. So that if at first both appear to be martyrs for the cause of their professions (and in both cases their professions seem to

the monstrous and the marvelous

have cosmical significance), they are in fact—as is the faceless boy of "The Child Who Raised Poisonous Snakes"—passive beings, buffeted by the weather of their own emaciated emotions. The Hunger Artist in the end becomes the sole witness to his own extremity; the seduction of morbidity is limited after all, and the interest evoked by monstrosity difficult to sustain. For the Snake Keeper and the Hunger Artist, the place for demonstration of their "finest form" is not in the land of the living. These two perform *for Eternal Night*.

Like Kafka, Can Xue proposes that the world is an illusion of mind. If the legs of the Hunger Artist scrape a ground that is *not really solid*, the Recorder, recording the inside of his own mind, only *sees emptiness ahead*. The dream he longs to record, the one that will evoke his own necessary and impossible dream, *is not forthcoming*. In desperation he looks to the sky where *there was nothing*. Yet he continues to wait for *a dreamland that had never yet been described, one charged with heat and blinding light*. Perhaps because those who might share the essential dream realize that the Recorder does not give a fig for them but only for his own reticent reverie, they pass him by. The Recorder watches them, his heart pulsing regularly *between hope and disappointment*. With inspired and cunning irony, Can Xue writes:

> And their dreamlands were nothing out of the ordinary, although they were filled with the mad joy of wandering in the vast universe; or with the conceitedness of a person who locks himself inside a cave deep within the shell of the earth, or with the horror of being captured by some beast of prey; or with the ghastly feeling of being in the process of dying. However, no one ever dreamed the image that appeared in the Recorder's mind.

(*This essay was inspired by the monstrous and the marvelous, and is dedicated to one of its exemplars: Harry Mathews.*)

Allegory by Randall Heath, 1997

THE DEATH CUNT OF DEEP DELL

Just a few months ago, a friend, knowing I was writing a novel in which the Marquis de Sade figures as a central character,[1] gave me a copy of *Salo*, Pasolini's great film based on Sade's *120 Days of Sodom*. In the film, Sade's libertines are fascists and Silling castle, Salo Mussolini's northern Italian holdout. Unlike Sade's exhausting encyclopaedic novel—a novel so deadly tiresome even its author found it unreadable—Pasolini's film is a great work even if it is almost impossible to watch it all the way through. If I mention *Salo* here, as a means to introduce this essay, it is because the film's most terrifying and unforgettable characters are the leering women brought to entertain the kidnappers and their victims with obscene stories. These storytellers reveal what is wrong with Sade's novel: in fetters the imagination is a dead and deadly thing. Sade's *120 Days* is not, as one might think, the work of an unbridled imagination, but of a mind bound by the imperious and fetishic (and, therefore, *limited*) exigencies of masturbatory fantasy.

Salo's storytellers do not evoke erotic response but revulsion; their stories are deadly because they are tedious, without wit or imagination. And they are didactic: their purpose is to teach the victims that sex is nothing more than a fatal machine, Nature's machine: blind, gravity-bound and implacable.

---

1. *The Fan-Maker's Inquisition*, Henry Holt, New York, 1999.

Interestingly, Pasolini's film is far darker than Sade's novel. *The 120 Days* is at times illuminated by a ferocious self-mockery and—if one has the patience (and the stomach) to read the thing in its entirety—it opens up, here and there, with displays of a kind of *noir* slapstick. (A priest, happy as a clam in a barrel of shit comes to mind.) Yet, Pasolini's storytellers are always smiling. Dressed to the nines like the good fairy of Oz, they, who are the enemy of humor, are, like skulls, eternally grinning.

Pasolini's storytellers introduce the idea of the Death Cunt, a gnostical perception of the female body as seduction, a lethal detour of the spirit leading to enslavement: the cunt as snare, prison, and coffin. In my essay "Optical Terror," I show how for Swift, woman *is* fatality. And if the Death Cunt palpitates at the heart of Sade and winks at the bottom of every Swiftian chamber pot, she shows up in Lewis Carroll's *Alice* (recall the Red Queen's lust for heads). And she haunts Kafka's *Castle*, too. An example: shortly after K arrives at the village inn, a massive landlady appears in the doorway, utterly blocking it. This landlady is the first of many women (Klamm's mistress Frieda, whom K fucks in puddles of beer, is another) who will be strewn across K's path like so many obstacles, so many death wishes.

Unexamined, the fear of the other is always destructive to individuals and to nations. Clitoridectomy and the current situation in Afghanistan—both examples of what can only be called a war against women—are expressions of such superstitious fear taken to extremes. If the roots of this essay are political and philosophical, and have informed my reading of Kafka and Swift (and I should add *The Tale of Gengi*, too: all those famished female spirits!), the idea of the Death Cunt has been useful in approaching the film and fiction of the following contemporaries who have engaged it in full awareness, and playfully: David Lynch (whose self-hating Laura[2] in the notorious TV

---

2. There's a great moment in *Twin Peaks* when a virgin has been dressed up in ruffles and bows and laid out on a brothel bed like Sleeping Beauty or Snow White; the crones who have dressed her scurry off cackling in a scene worthy of Coover or Angela Carter.

the monstrous and the marvelous

series *Twin Peaks* is another version of the theme); the Brothers Quay, whose filmed theaters of objects bristle with unexpected instants of dark eroticism; the often imitated and inimitable Robert Coover, for whom the Death Cunt is both ubiquitous and a species of talisman; and Angela Carter, who proposes it as an emblem of Revenge. Angela, no longer with us, who continues to enchant us.

1. David Lynch

I cherish a particularly eerie moment in David Lynch's *Eraserhead* when a radiator metamorphoses into a miniature theater and an excessively sentimentalized Thumbelina performs in the void. As lively as she looks, she is an illusion, a lethal figment of the mind. Her stage is set in the dark heart of psychotic and sidereal space, and to see her is to be both mortal and mad. The larval boy who evokes her is as much a phantom as she; it is unclear who dreams whom, although it is likely a lesser archon is dreaming them both. One of the Death Cunt's many disguises, she will return in the shape of some barely roasted birds, which when carved, evoke fecal fucking, and again as Lula's fatal mother in *Wild at Heart*.

In *Blue Velvet*, the Death Cunt takes the shape of a vertical, toothed mouth, painted red and whispering "Hit me." Soon after, it is suspended like a hideous gris-gris over apprentice sleuth Jeffrey Beaumont's bed. The mouth belongs to torch singer Dorothy Vallens, who by getting Jeffrey to hit her, compromises his humanity as well as her own. When Jeffrey tells Sandy, his girl, "I'm seeing something that was always hidden," it is the Death Cunt he has seen: that "Slow Club." And when Frank, the psychopath, takes Jeffrey and Dorothy on a joy ride to "Pussy Heaven," they land up in Hell. As Frank beats Jeffrey in the stomach and face and Dorothy writhes in terror, A Death Cunt from Pussy Heaven bumps and grinds on the hood of Frank's car.

The Death Cunt burns at the core of *Wild at Heart* as Lula's fatal mother. Here Lynch's version of the Death Cunt is not unlike Manuel Puig's in *Kiss of the Spider Woman*, a great novel truffled with cinematic femmes fatales: Irena, the panther woman who kills a canary simply by putting her hand into its cage, and the mother of the revolutionary, Valentin, who has been sleeping with the man responsible for Valentin's arrest. Valentin's mother is fucking the enemy, just as Lula's mother in *Wild at Heart* is fucking the man who killed Lula's father, as well as the man who intends to kill Lula's lover, Sailor — and she is the instigator of both crimes. Later, the Death Cunt takes the bloated shape of three pornographic graces poisoning the evening air of Greater Tuna — Lynch's rural vision of Hell — and the obscene villain Bobby's anal mouth that sullies, but does not destroy, the morally free Lula. And when Bobby's woman slides across the screen like a white-hot snake — a blonde Isabella Rosselini — it is clear her hole and her house are simply another version of the Devil's den so central to *Lost Highway*.

The Death Cunt reaches quintessence in *Lost Highway*'s "Deep Dell," the address of the producer of snuff films — in the acutely eroticized "glamours" Alice and Renée — spawn of the Devil's cunt-cabin (which is also the Devil's own ubiquitous eye). The Cabin recalls *Wild at Heart*'s house on fire, the little shack in *Blue Velvet* that stands near the place where Jeffrey finds the severed ear, and *Blue Velvet*'s "Deep River Apartments." It also brings to mind Robert Coover's Technicolor take on the fairy-tale gingerbread house with its irresistible, cherry-red genital door. Like Hansel, Lynch's doubled hero of *Lost Highway* can't stay away. The devil has fucked his mind; teased to lunacy, his only means of escape is to atomize.

Despite its moments of intense weirdness, *Lost Highway* is not anywhere near as good as *Blue Velvet* or *Wild at Heart*. The latter is wildly romantic without being sentimental, and also very sexy. If Lula's mother is the Death Cunt par excellence, Laura Dern's Lula is a Life Cunt; she's hot and she's funny. *Lost Highway*, on the other hand, is often downright silly, except for Bill Pullman's haunted performance and the fabulous

Patricia Arquette's Alice and Renée. You can see they are both nothing but fang and flame, but they are impossible *not* to watch. They are the whore of Babylon, the one who brought Enkidu down.

"Do you want to fuck me?" asks the Devil as Alice. "Do you want to ask me *why?*"

2. Quay Brothers

In the many versions of the sumptuous Sumerian epic *Gilgamesh* (and they are all beautiful), the Death Cunt appears as Shamhat, a harlot sent by Gilgamesh, the king of Uruk, into the Cedar Woods to seduce his rival, the savage but godlike, starlike Enkidu—who has never known love—and bring him down. Shamhat shows Enkidu her naked body and she *shows him the things a woman knows how to do* [Ferry's translation]; *for six days and seven nights Enkidu groans over her* [Kovacs] and then, in every version, he is so weakened by the encounter he can barely move. It is as if *life had left his body* [Mason]; as if his body *was bound . . . with a cord* [Sandars].

The Quays' Enkidu (from *A Largely Disguised Reduction of the Epic of Gilgamesh*) is lost embracing the promise of erotic delight. Prison cell and torture chamber, Gilgamesh's little house is suspended in limbo, ruled by rage, and like *Lost Highway's* Devil's cabin, inescapable. Drawn like a moth to flame, Enkidu leaves the safety of the Cedar Woods to enter it and examine Gilgamesh's dazzling poison damsel. Her peepshow genital is deep pink, a color another dreamer of satanic houses, Jean Ray, calls *bastard red, the color of shame* and, when it engenders a universe—Ray's version of Coover's Big Bang—*the pink catalyst.* Overcome by the female seduction of space-time (her sex is also a pendulum) Enkidu leans into her, springing the trap. He is seized, suspended in the air with wires. (In the original story, Enkidu gets to lie with the whore for seven nights before attempting to rise and finding he is as though tied down.)

rikki ducornet

Immobilized by the gorgeous stuff of dreams—a bolt of orange silk is here a marvelous metaphor for the seductions of the illusory material world—Enkidu is brutally beaten by Gilgamesh, and his wings cut from his body. The deadly dream theater has now become a cage. Gilgamesh—a species of conquistador fused to the body of his horse—maniacally circles his prisoner on his compulsive little wheels.

Lucent in the Quay's other masterpiece, *The Street of Crocodiles*, the Death Cunt reappears in the form of a pocket watch, a dressmaker's dummy and a hairy glove—seductive artifacts of a world held together by spit and string. Space and time are both so old and shoddy they are barely able to sustain the illusion of the real. By film's end the empty-headed tailor-archons of the world's dusty rag and bone shop, having exhausted their short supply of sumptuous matter, are overtaken by entropy.

3. Robert Coover: Kabalistic Dada

In Robert Coover's chronically ambiguous Comedies of Terror, chaos is exemplified by a cosmical ogress too; a Charybdis animated by opposites, she cannibalizes everything that moves. Coover engages the archetypal femme fatale, the Kabala, and even the techniques of Dada cinema to create disturbingly kaleidoscopic (and Kali-scopic) fictions in which the Death Cunt (his term) plays a central role.

Dada was the infant of calamity, and its primary images were recurrently catastrophic. By propelling images into one another, by calamatizing *idées reçues*, Dada delighted in disorder, demonstrating in a most tangible way Coover's irresistible gnostical argument: *calamity is the normal circumstance of the universe* ("Phantom of the Movie Palace").

Like the Kabala,[3] Dada revealed the rents in the fabric of things

---

3. Long before Picabia, the Kabalist Abulafia, another "aristocrat of disorder," created a mystical method of free association which consisted of *jumping or skipping* from one idea to another. He abstracted words from thoughts and meditated upon the singular images in suspension. Thoughts, images and words were atomised by Abulafia's technique.

and more: it argued that the world's fabric was itself made of absences. Cinema, then Dada, and above all Dada cinema, conveyed the vertiginous fact of porosity; if, once again, the world was flat, the edge of Yahweh's footstool bobbing like a cork above chaos (a Kabalistic notion), it was also a sieve world riddled with holes. As Coover proposes in *A Night at the Movies*, the mystic veil has metamorphosed into a movie screen, and the expanding universe has been reduced to *a gleaming thicket of tangled film spooling out . . . like some monstrous birth*, animated by light motes passing through a Kabalistic window, igniting for an instant only in the air.

Shrinking and expanding, anorexic and bulimic, Coover's universe seesaws (now you see it, now you don't) upon a cinematic *dream cloth—the nothing happening faster and faster*. (Recall how toward dawn in *Gerald's Party*, the kitchen, seemingly empty, is in fact actively engaged in extensive cooking. In Picabia's words: *There is only one movement and that is perpetual motion*.)

If the cosmos is a kitchen and a light show, it is a cunt as well, a Death Cunt to which the poet (impotent, potent) sings his pricksongs—hopeful, lustful, sorry and absurd—all the while meditating upon the *Everlasting Wound*, the *purview* (the pussyview of what's to come); it is her vulva seesawing just behind the veil:

> He pokes around in the wings with a kind of lustful terror, hoping to find what he most fears to find. He kicks at the tassels and furbelows of the grand drapery, flounces the house curtains and travelers, examines the screen: is there a hole in it?

Like sex, art is an attempt to fill the void, *to fill the silence* ("The Gingerbread House"). *The miracle of artifice is miracle enough* ("The Phantom of the Movie Palace"), and surely the only "miracle" we have.

Spooked as he may be, the poet's pricksong is a lovesong nonetheless. Coover's Pan, named Morris, offers this ditty:

> Her hairs was black as silver snails
> Her teeth was white as gold
> The copse was green as nightingales
> The runlet fresh as mold
> The runlet fresh as mold . . .

This song could have been sung for the rotting wife in "The Marker," whose *lips are black and her blonde hair, now long and tangled . . . splayed out over the pillow like a urinal mop spread out to dry.* A fitting song too, for Sade's "Dulcinea" of *The 120 Days*, who offers: *an ancient, yellow and shriveled body, dry, shapeless, and unfleshed, the full description whereof, irrespective of your particular fancies in such matters, would so fill you with horror it were better for me to say no more . . .*

Albeit perpetual, hopeful and ubiquitous, the pricksong is random, a *thoughtless childish habit* ("The Gingerbread House") and as ineffectual as a *balling of crumbs, a kneading, a coaxing, a pinching—as if for luck or pleasure.* If crumbs are wasted, *so then is the story.* But the singer cannot help himself; if to sing is to exorcise, to *conceal,* to *entertain,* it is also to conjure. His heart, you see, belongs to Kali. Beauty, hag, corpse, princess, witch, baby-sitter, and fairy, it is She who rules all wands, pockets, and keys. A garland of rotting heads hung from Her neck, the fruit of desire in Her hand—*a soft radiant pulsing* ("The Gingerbread House"), She breaks the ribs of the real as She prompts an impressive erection. *Fucking corpse* and *lily-white goosegirl reeking of pogonias,* the Blue Fairy and the Virgin Mary, She is also *a kind of walking light show:*

> Her cheeks seem to pop alight like his Café American sign each time the
> airport beacon sweeps past, shifting slightly like a sequence of film frames.
> Time itself may be like that, he knows: not a ceaseless flow, but a rapid
> series of electrical leaps across tiny gaps between discontinuous bits.
> ("You Must Remember This")

the monstrous and the marvelous

~

The Death Cunt's aspects are innumerable: it is *a door . . . shaped like a heart . . . as red as a cherry, always half open* ("The Gingerbread House"); it is a *holey altar: "You just kneel down and kiss it, honey!"* ("Intermission"). It is a *corral of sorrows* ("Shoot out at Gentry's Junction"), a *grave* and a *tattered loop* ("After Lazarus"); it is the *revenge of Something-or-Other* ("The Phantom of the Movie Palace"), a *maze of probable improbability, a far door ajar* ("Charlie in the House of Rue") and, again, a *door banging in the wind* ("Lap Dissolves"). It is an *airless prairie, a kind of thick muddy wall with rubbery teats, a putrid dike holding back the real world (of light!); a barricade of bone, a vast immobile shithouse.* It is a *cauldron as big as a bathtub* (Briar Rose); It is *heart-shaped and bloodstone red, its burnished surface gleaming in the sunlight . . . shining like a ruby, like hard cherry candy, and pulsing softly, radiantly. Yes, marvelous! Delicious! Insuperable! But beyond: what is that sound of black rags flapping?* ("The Gingerbread House").

Come full circle, we return to the *ghabghab*, the sacrificial pit—that primal place of terror. The cosmical orifice bristles with thorns!

> *She has told her (the little dimwit has forgotten this, perhaps she will tell it again) about the prince who, trapped in the briars, was given three wishes and wasted them by first wishing himself in Beauty's bedroom, which he found empty, then wishing to know where she was, and, on learning she was in the very hedge he'd been trapped in, wishing himself back in the briars again, though the wishes weren't completely wasted because at least now, on a clear day when their shouts carried, he had company in his suffering* ("Briar Rose").

~

The twentieth century may be exemplary in its obsession with absences, missing links, black holes—astronomical, sexual and psychological. Our literature is truffled with allusions to the world's illusory and particulated nature: Borges' craps game played out in a latrine named Quafqua, Kafka's holey empire, Beckett's Godot, Krap's last tape, Coover's colander movie screen, Calvino's Comics, Bowles' North Africa, Carter's dream machines, and so on. These fictions are all takes on Babel, which should not surprise us; never has the random nature of things been more in evidence, nor the gap between words and their meanings, greater. And if Borges' craps players imitate Divine Disorder, Coover tramps about in it delightedly in ten-league boots, and with the tramp's wistfulness: if only masculine space could fill feminine[4] time!

> He recognizes in all these dislocations . . . his lonely quest for the impossible mating, the crazy embrace of polarities as though the distance between his terror and the comedy of the void was somehow erotic — it's a kind of pornography. ("The Phantom of the Movie Palace") It's almost as though two completely different places, two completely different times, are being forced to mesh, to intersect where no intersection is possible, causing a kind of warp in the universe. ("You Must Remember This")

This kind of warp, this kind of pornography, is charted by Coover's treatment of a Chaplin short schematized as a chapter of accidents; Coover organizes the material into an animated exquisite corpse. Like the Quays' and Lynch's hungry houses, Coover's House of Rue contains pits and pendulums; clocks, like cunts, split open, their works springing out like wild hairs. The cinematic house, which like a clock can be rewound, is also a sorcerer's-apprentice world of waters, flooded by soup, douchebag, ink, alcohol and tears. And like the incessant yet insufficient light in Borges' library of Babel, the House of Rue is aglitter with bright, sourceless light. It illuminates some emblematic pies.

In a hybrid nightmare of Kabalistic Dada, a toreador maid metamorphosed into a flickering lightbulb (a beacon suggesting gnosis)

---

4. The coffin lid is opening! ("Charlie in the House of Rue").

the monstrous and the marvelous

beckons the knob of Charlie's cock into her lethal closet. *A black shaggy patch of pubic hair*[5] conceals her holey terror. (And the name of God. His name is: *Hungry all the time.*) And we are left with a Holey Trinity of terrible Questions:

> *What kind of place is this? Who took the light away? And why is everybody laughing?*

4. A Scatological and Cannibal Clock: Angela Carter's "The Fall River Ax Murders" and "The Loves of Lady Purple"

At the center of Lizzie Borden's story, the sun's vortex gyres; it is, turn by turn, a Catherine's wheel, the unstoppable face of a clock, the mouth of Moloch, the mouth of an ogress, a furnace, an anus, and a vexing mirror that, like a hangman's noose, mercilessly distorts the features.

Automatons, the Bordens—all freaks, extremes of nature, the sins of avarice, gluttony, and anger personified—ambulate within the abridged universe of a clockwork house. Wound to a frenzy, they rotate about the dark hole of Lizzie's rage in an ever-diminishing orbit.

Like Saint Catherine, Lizzie is emblematic and exemplary; she is reduced to sign—the ax she carries within her grinding madly. In fact, Lizzie is the other side of Catherine's coin, the dark face of the moon: she is the Saint's negative. Her raptures lead not to Heaven but to Hell. In place of a halo Lizzie Borden wears a chamber pot. And like that other emblematic female, Red Riding Hood ("A Company of Wolves"), Lizzie is bleeding. The menstrual cycle, the ticking clock, the factory siren, the sun, the moon, and the chamber pot are all reminders of mortality.

Upon her room's revolving stage, Lizzie makes a *planetary round*. (And here I cannot help but recall a possible pun on *axis* and *axes* uncov-

---

5. Her fur below.

ered in *Alice*, that is, the Red Queen's viciously cycled obsession with axing off heads.) An infernal teetotum spelled upon a wheeling stage, Lizzie keeps herself indoors as if she were a piece of photosensitive paper; she would remain white, unimpressed by the dark man she has conjured and who she believes circles the house relentlessly. (Lizzie is much like that other murderous puppet of Carter's—Lady Purple. Part Kali, part Erzsebet Bathory, Lady Purple, too, has been made monstrous by the voracity of others. She, too, is *all twang, all tension*.)

Infernal machine, a circus ring that offers the devil's own dancing dogs (Sirius, along with sun and moon, blazes down upon this cosmical theater), Spindle City and the Borden homestead are contained within a magic circle, transmogrified into things so small as to fit in Old Borden's pocket. Lizzie has been *spelled*, reduced to dead. Self-repeating, her soul in bandages, she paces the coffin house like a perambulating mummy. (So coffinlike is the house, that *the maid lies on her back . . . in case she dies during the night. . . .*) And this *spelling* refers to Morse code, to the coded messages that tattoo murderous demands upon Lizzie's brain—perhaps the ghostly drumming of vanished aborigines who have cursed the land with madness and death. Finally, Lizzie's stepmother *oppressed her like a spell*. If Lizzie escapes briefly to Europe, the trip is but a *round trip*, and any news of abroad ripped into squares *so that they can wipe their arses . . .*

Lizzie suffers *peculiar spells when her mind misses a beat*. Curious *lapses of consciousness . . . which often . . . come at the time of her menses*. The *sputtering radiance* which *emanates from everything* recalls the sputtering City Hall clock. At such moments, the very birds that sit in the trees are reduced to clockwork: *whirring, clicking and chucking like no birds known before*. And we are given the marvelous image of time halved like an apple: *time opened in two*. Time's halved apple affords a species of fractured gnosis, an *over-clarity*. Within the fracture, when the world stutters and Lizzie's brain misses a beat, a burglary takes place and a safe is assaulted with a pair of scissors. Old Borden confuses private property with private parts and is *a man raped*. To break the spell of evil fortune, he locks his

the monstrous and the marvelous

rooms for luck and expands his holdings by constructing a brick build-
ing the size of a city block (but this will not prevent his own block
from being knocked off in the end. He will lie in his coffin headless,
Lizzie's gold ring orbiting his little finger.)[6]

Emperor of the City of Spindles, Old Borden is Capital as Coffin
Maker, Grim Reaper, Time's Passing. He is both undertaker and hearse.
The only thing Edenic in the wasteland of his making is a pear tree laden
with fruit which he *waters with his own urine*. Time is money, and both spell
Death. Like salmonella, emblems proliferate, and suddenly Old Borden
and his fat wife embody Appetite; the gingerbread house and all within
it are threatened by that bottomless pit: Mrs. Borden's mouth. If Time
and Heat have thus far ruled the day, Meat joins in at noon creating a
diabolic trinity whose holy of holies is the chamber pot—a necro-
mancer's mirror of *merde* which reflect a flux of apocalyptic associations.
Household objects rise to the surface of a *queasy water*; the master bed-
room is a *wunderkammer* of domestic horrors which includes the mystic
implements of Mrs. Borden's *toilette: a bone comb missing three teeth and lightly
threaded with grey hairs* and *a hairpiece curled up like a dead squirrel*.

Consider for a moment that squirrel and that comb. Skull-like,
the comb is missing teeth, just as Lizzie's mind misses beats. The comb
represents mortality (comb and hairpiece comprising an impoverished
vanitas); a comb *sans* teeth could be an emblem of stuttering time.
Curled up, the squirrel is simultaneously fetal and dead (Lizzie's own
menses are all for naught); it creates a snarling vortex, a cingulum of
sorts, a noose. (This *nature morte* prefigures the list of burgled objects
which include Mrs. Borden's collar necklace and her watch!)

And now, the house, an architectural infamy—built like a squirrel cage or a revolving door, spelled, smelling of menstrual blood and
sweat—is reduced by the rotary mouth of the ogress stepmother to a
prodigious body of mortal evidence: it fumes.

---

6. The Bordens' skulls were sent to Harvard for examination.

rikki ducornet   93

If at the house's center an anus rages and mouth, an inventory of sound, like so many gaseous bodies in orbit, will return as inevitably as sun, moon, and mutton (like the cow of nursery rhyme, the mutton, quite *high* enough to jump over the moon, will return to the table morning, noon, and night): *hot, fire, sputter, stutter* (Lizzie's hair, crackling with static, stutters too); *heat, meat, eat.*[7]

Excessive appetite and *copious purges* gyre and gimble until Lizzie cuts loose and *the eaters become the meal.* Within the house of ginger-bread, appetite is the only thing *not kept within confinement.* Not only is Mrs. Borden's appetite prodigious, Old Borden *would gobble up the city of Fall River.*

A constant confusion is sustained between mentally and physically ingesting and digesting, between mouth and anus, coffin and house, pockets, chamber pots and clocks. The Bordens are likened to the Sprats who, as you will recall, licked the platter clean. In other words, they left Lizzie nothing with which to satisfy her hunger. She is not an eater but is instead eaten away by anger and the gnashing of her bleeding womb. This anger has made her supernatural; if she has *the jaws of a concentration camp attendant* and the eyes of Red Riding Hood's wolf, she is in fact a werewolf ruled by the moon. We even catch a glimpse of her howling.

Clocks are central to the tale, and the Borden dining room contains a very special clock intriguingly silent. Recall what Lewis Carroll had to say about stopped clocks: *they are right twice a day.* Even when time stands still, history repeats itself: *A stopped clock of black marble, shaped like a Greek mausoleum, stood on the sideboard, becalmed. Father stood at the head of the table and shaved the meat.*

The father standing at the head of the Greek table is Jupiter who, because he feared his offspring with Metis would be more exalted

---

7. Again, I think of Alice: the tea party in orbit. The Bordens are a syzygy—sun, earth, and moon in alignment.

than he, devoured her. After, he suffered such acute pain he told Vulcan to split his head open. Armed and fully grown, Minerva leaped from her father's brain.

The story is revelatory. Children of Freud, we know that Lizzie, motherless and eaten, is Old Borden's brain child. By cleaving her father's head, she gives birth to her full-grown self. And we know, without being told, that Lizzie's *dark man* is a figment of her mind; that the scatological burglar who fouls Old Borden's bed is none other than Lizzie herself. (We can appreciate, also, that Borden's factory chimney was the tallest for its time in the United States!)

Finally, to return to Saint Catherine: Catherine's wheel was set with razors. Just as her body was placed upon it and made to spin, the wheel broke apart with such violence the razors reeled into the crowd hacking limbs and slitting throats.[8]

The coloring of this domestic apocalypse must be crude and the *design profoundly simplified for the maximum emblematic effect.*

~

"The Loves of Lady Purple" unfolds at a fair, a fragment of the *original fair*—a dark kernel of compressed matter that blew apart *long ago in a diaspora of the amazing.* The implication is Manichean: matter is corrupt: *Here, the grotesque is the order of the day.*

We are in Transylvania—the spawning ground of famished freaks—and Lady Purple, *monstrous goddess of unappeasable appetites* embodies what Sade revealed: revenge is the answer to mortification. *Queen of Night* and poison damsel, Lady Purple, who brings to mind Hungary's "Bloody Countess" Erzsebet Bathory, Kali (with her flute made from her lover's thighbone), and Sade's Juliette, performs in a

---

8. If the Palladium—the clockword statue of Pallas Athena (Minerva)—did not carry an ax or a wheel, she did carry a pike and a *spindle.*

puppet booth of gothic capacities where anything is possible because *here only the marvelous exists* (and this includes everything monstrous). The theater is her carriage of fire; it is the slumbering world's burning mirror. And if Puppet Master and assistants have made a pact with silence and do not name the unnamable, the rites they perform are in Her name: Bane and Terrible Enlightenment.

As was Lizzie Borden, Lady Purple is motherless, a robber, an arsonist, and a parenticide. The smile she wears is fixed: the smile of Blue Beard; the smile of the tiger. (In another of Carter's fables, "Master," the mortified slave transmogrifies into a tiger and devours her tormentor. The theme central to these tales is not so much Death and the Maiden, but the enraged maiden *as* Death.) Lady Purple's voice, like *fur soaked in honey,* conjures Sacher Masoch's Venus (and Gregor Samsa's photograph of the young woman swaddled in furs).

Pornography, Carter writes in *The Sadian Woman, involves an abstraction of human intercourse in which the self is reduced to its formal elements. These are the redundant abstractions scratched into latrine walls: the prong and fringed hole; that dumb mouth from which the teeth have been pulled.*

Death Cunt and Emblem of Revenge, Carter's Lady Purple has all her teeth and then some. Indeed, so good is this object on strings at objectifying others, that in the end her "Master" is reduced to dry sticks; the kindling which feeds the fire that consumes him.

SORTILEGE

Mary Caponegro offers fiction of a vivid and exalted weirdness. One leaves her stories as one awakens from an important if disquieting dream, the symbols of which—one is certain— are invocatory formulas, potent and cryptic at the same time, and powerful enough to dispel psychological sickness, perhaps, or reveal the true, if terrifying, nature of the world. Once again she has written a wonderful collection, *Five Doubts*, a book that is also beautifully conceived *as an object*, its illustrations taken from Etruscan tomb paintings, Sicilian mosaics, and the early works of Leonardo. Altogether admirable, "An Etruscan Catechism" and "Tambola" are two stories that particularly captured my attention.

1. "An Etruscan Catechism"

The magical inspection of entrails has its origin in the Middle East. The Babylonians claimed that haruspication was the invention of the gods, and that the passions were housed not in the heart, but the liver. There is, in the Italian city of Piacenza[1] a liver of bronze, a model from which the apprentice haruspex of Etruria learned the art of reading, in the livers of sheep, the causes of mortality and other disasters, and to discover the intentions of gods now mercifully silent.

---

1. Unlike in France, where they have been reduced to devils and drainpipes, the ancient gods appear to flourish in Italy, and this thanks to the persistence of Etruscan influence.

rikki ducornet   97

The bronze liver of Piacenza indicates the organ's four principal chambers, including the gall bladder, the *processus papielaris* and a pyramidal projection called the *processus pyramidalis.*[2] The entire surface is inscribed with the uniquely inscrutable language of Etruria. *The whole of the liver's houses' sum is forty-four, and each is affiliated with particular gods in the heavens.*

"An Etruscan Catechism" opens with the haruspex's plow unearthing the humbled form of the god Tages who, as he emerges from the clods, *like a beetle or worm*—and both are vermin partial to corpses—thrusts the book of Sacred Law upon the reader's gaze. Tages, with his infant's face, dwarf's body and old man's head, is exemplary of *the force of strangeness* [that] *drives the world.* Caponegro next calls up Etruria's sixteen gods, indicates the "house" each claims on the freshly harvested organ's riddled surface, and describes their dubious powers. All things, remarkable and unremarkable, are in their management and evolve beneath their persistent shadow: *An Etruscan cannot avoid the will of the gods.* It is soon evident that if the haruspex *is never in error,* if his pointy hat *connects us to heaven,* his knowledge is distressingly futile; the warm liver he fingers with such intimacy affords no safety. One infers that it would provide greater service fried up with onions.

A number of compelling facts or series of commotions are offered, tumbled together and recurring as an infinite and mutable set with obsessive constancy or inevitability: Tages rising from the furrow, a man *in the center of a collision from both ends* "plowed" by another as he faces the horns of a charging bull; a man blinded by a hood and attacked by a dog driven by its master; sheeplike ciphers submitting to slaughter; an Etruscan beauty in her horned tomb, having fatally collided with time, and surrounded by a clutter of abortive potencies as powerless, in fact, as the gold she carries in her mouth. "An Etruscan Catechism" is also a *vanitas:*

---

2. Could the practice of harupsication have influenced architecture?

the monstrous and the marvelous

At times, he might hear voices such as this: O haruspex, I seek your
counsel: tell me, if you hear, what sector of which god's will has led me to
this place? What is its name? All is familiar yet I feel unmoored, unsure.
Shall I have my parasol in my tomb? My comb, how many mirrors,
haruspex? My lovely boxes of cosmetics in the shape of beasts? My
earrings? Bracelets? Diadem? Will it ever again be warm enough to
warrant my unfolding the fan folded into this wall of my tomb, my tomb,
like some vertical table which houses familiar objects that comfort? Am I
one among the dead then? When will life turned to death turn again?
Will it turn to the Styx and return me from that brackish mirror to gaze
in the one whose polished surface will offer a woman some centuries older,
whose hair worn in ringlets, is now worn in braids, whose hair is coiled
round, whose myths etched in bronze on the backs of these mirrors have
entertained her for all the hours she spent of her lives braiding or coiling
or curling, adorning neck and wrists, fastening jewelry and painting her
face more often than not for the man who once done with the nubile
obliging servants would find her again in the bed, interrupting her
reading, to read all the lines of her flesh. And she said to him often, I
confess to you now, "your hands are so knowing so gentle, if I loved the
Etruscans my people more than my own pleasure I would insist you enter
the vocation of the haruspex, caressing the liver of sheep after sheep as
intently, as tenderly, sensuously as you caress me."

~

Each figure in the tableaux proposed is, at some point or other,
and, as is the god Tages, *a hybrid creature*: the two men joined in
embrace, the man transformed by the hood, the painted corpse: all
conjure up mutability.[3] In constant flux, gods, animals and things erupt:

---

3. The Etruscans wore horned helmets, making of themselves chimeras, evoking,
   simultaneously, the phallus, the bull, and the moon.

one head sprouts snakes, another a second head; an entire goddess is excreted by yet another; the gods' ejaculate spills across the sky; the silent organs of sheep grow in the dark only to be harvested again and again, like fruit or flowers. The tombs of Etruria are hybrids, and they erupt, too. Containing rafters and cooking pots, they recall the tombs of Mesopotamia and Babylon, with their bull heads of mud plaster thrusting through the chamber walls. Chatal Huyuk foretells the Grotta Bella of Cervetri: *how curious to find a wall tumescent instead of flat.* The banquet couch, so gaily depicted in the frescoes of the tombs, is now—for all Etrurians—a sarcophagus: *that hard bed.* Standing above the beauty's corpse the haruspex fingers, as is his wont, a fresh liver. He is overwhelmed by the clotted complexities of things and by a dreadful certainty that the *very gold that crowns her teeth will one day, after Etruscans are no longer, be extracted like a liver from a sheep.* His pointy hat affords no powers nor protections; like the lion in another story, "The Spectacle," he is *surrounded and invaded* all at once. Time and space are beyond interpretation; the gods' bloody and palpable texts are erroneous.

2. "Tombola"

The Italian game of *tombole* is played with colorful boards divided into "houses"[4] as well, and each also contains an exemplary figure: the Virgin Mary, an old man, a soldier, a child receiving a spanking, Pulcinella, a hunchback, a good woman, a bad woman, a leg of mutton, a necklace, a bottle of wine. These take on significance as their number is called; the random order of their prominence proposes a new reading within the structure of Caponegro's narrative, a new "scheme of things." But no matter who the central figure may be: thief, boy, shopkeeper, mafioso, or drunk, and no matter the elements that give the tale its shape—chamber pot, bowl of soup, cat, or wheel of cheese—the

---

4. Mary Caponegro informs me that in her experience, the tokens used to mark these are pieces of dried orange peel.

tombola's lightning glimpses of possible itineraries evoke the tomb too.

> *The balls of the lieutenant are as much a piece of meat as the legs of Lily,*
> *just ask the hunchback.*

Like "An Etruscan Catechism," "Tombola" is a *vanitas*; its thirty-three narratives are each punctuated by a dark "seeing": of lice, a knife, a chamber pot, a deadly sin and the hunchback—his deformity making of him a "hybrid" significant of "glamours":

> *I will beat you if you stare at the crazy man, says his mother, saddled*
> *already with a brood of children, or if you go in the nasty weather*
> *without your hat. For dinner you will eat only bread, and be lucky to*
> *find a bride, if you continue to insist on using these naughty words, think*
> *of nothing but tits and ass, and Beppino, I gaze in astonishment at what*
> *was made of my own flesh and blood, that seems instead the work of*
> *devils. By the lieutenant's balls, I don't know what to do with you. The*
> *death that speaks.*

And:

> *There is blood in the garden. It does not come from under the signorina's*
> *skirt, that mysterious place which sees always the earth, nor from the*
> *sacrament. There is death and there is sudden senseless death by someone*
> *else's hand. But have a glass of wine, forget it, dream of the lovely mouth*
> *of the wicked woman, watch the Pulcinella skit. Pray to St. Anthony for*
> *the mind you lost, and be grateful that you live in Italy. Buy some*
> *roasted chestnuts on the street, even though they cost, don't knock over the*
> *chamberpot so distracted are you by the image of her mouth. But what*
> *death makes sense? says that sensuous suddenly disquieting hole.*

∾

The Italian word for tomb robber is *tombarolo;* the gambler, in his way, is a robber also, attempting to cheat fate by stealing instants of hope. Winning makes the gambler a lucky man, luckier for a moment than his neighbor. A win appears to overcome the impositions and limitations the fates impose, to alter the world's dark discourse, to indulge, if all too briefly, irrational thoughts of escape.

The peak of the Etruscan haruspex's hat is the place where gods and men meet, a curious point of conjunction; the tombola's houses of brightly colored rooms are where the fates—in the shapes of a knife, a noose and a pistol—convene.

> *With my hand I fire the cannon, with my knife I eat my hat. Don't listen to me, I'm a fool. What's got into my head? The weather is bad. Send me to prison where I can have a good cry, and grow old, like the woman who lives here where already I'm the master of the house, an old house, and your mother and I had you brood of kids instead of dancing around the fountain that we may as well run off in this terrible weather.*

the monstrous and the marvelous

BOOKS OF NATURE: THE POETRY OF CÉSAR VALLEJO AND THE BOXES OF JOSEPH CORNELL

Great poetry has the ability to pare language down to the bones and to crack those bones wide open. What is revealed is the *marrow* of language, the Adamic clay of Dreamtime which, when formed into words, spells worlds into being. Poetry is slaughter too: a tender slaughter. It reaches for the palpitating heart of things; it seeds our dreams with a bloody hail.

∼

Vallejo's poem "The Book of Nature," exemplifies such magic acts. Here a man, turn by turn professor, rector, expert in shouts, good student and ignoramus—is become the murmurous tree to which he speaks. Both the tree and the man are speechless and speaking, both dead and alive, quicksilver and dry stick. And both are in suspension between an *obvious* water—*obvious* because illuminated by the sun—and the sun itself which, in fact, illuminates nothing. Shining falsely in the water, the sun is a mere semblance, a parody of itself. As is the poet. As is the tree in whose dead leaves the poet, also a scholar, cannot read his destiny.

And the *false sun* is the three of hearts—the lover at the apex of a love triangle—a queen of diamonds who—even if she glitters—cannot be counted on to illuminate anything either.

The Book of Nature

    Professor of sobbing—I said to a tree—
stick of quicksilver, murmurous
linden, at the bank of the Marne, a good student
is reading in your deck of cards, in your dead foliage,
between the obvious water and the false sun,
his three of hearts, his queen of diamonds.

    Rector of the chapters of heaven,
of the ardent fly, of the manual calm there is in asses;
rector of deep ignorance, a bad student,
is reading in your deck of cards, in your dead foliage
the hunger for reason that maddens him
and the thirst for dementia that drives him wild.

    Expert in shouts, conscious tree, strong,
fluvial, double, solar, double, fanatic,
knowledgeable in the cardinal roses, totally
embedded, until blood spurts, in stingers, a student
is reading in your deck of cards, in your dead foliage,
his precocious, telluric, volcanic king of spades.

    Oh professor, from having been so ignorant!
Oh rector, from trembling so much in the air!
Oh expert, from so much bending over!
Oh linden! Oh stick murmuring by the Marne!
                        (Poem 149)

    Let us recall that at the heart of many of the world's cosmologies, the tree, a mystical organism, is the symbol of the body of God. A cosmic skeleton, its branches both hold the universe and reveal the complexity of its infinite reachings; its leaves are a shimmering Book of Splendor.

                                   the monstrous and the marvelous

The professor of sobbing—tree, stick and good student—is also rector of the chapters of heaven: chapters reduced to the buzzings of an ardent fly, to the silence of dumb beasts. Rector of deep ignorance, our stick-man is, in fact, Rector of Nothing: a dull-witted student. One wonders—is the foliage unreadable because he cannot decipher its message? Or are the leaves of Heaven's Book devoid of meaning? If hunger for reason drives the tree-man wild, nevertheless he thirsts for that madness because knowledge contains the possible promise of transcendence—as does love. Perhaps the Queen of Diamonds is here revealed as Sophia—she who exemplifies wisdom.

Expert in shouts, man, that conscious tree, is also a river (a molded river) and sun; he is *double*: the river of the first stanza and the false sun reflected therein. Fanatic because obsessed with love and wisdom, he is seized by red *flowers*—*cardinal* red—as in cardinal points and sins—which cover all directions—geographical and bookish—with their thorns. He is bleeding, stung, crucified, earthbound and volcanic (he is, if rooted to the ground, an *expert in shouts*) reading his own tree of life, his own particulated heart as best he can. A black king, spade in hand, he digs the earth for clues. Because, in Vallejo's universe, the clues are to be had in nature. Nature is simultaneously the source of language and the self. But the risk is *that from so much bending over*, the poet may miss the point. In the final strophe the poet sees himself as from a distance; expert in shouts he cries *Oh!* naming his own ignorance, his capacity to hang suspended in ether. We are left with a mere stick murmuring to itself, deluded by its own reflection, floating in a river of ignorance. Elsewhere Vallejo asks:

> *Speaking of kindling, do I silence the fire?*
> *Sweeping the ground, do I overlook the fossil?*
> (Poem 133)

In another poem, the poet

> *runs from everything . . . flees*
>> *directly to sob alone*
>>> (Poem 113)

And, again:

>> *. . . describe yourself as atmospheric, Being of*
>>> *smoke,*
>> *in the double time step of a skeleton.*
>>> (Poem 161, [McShine 33])

In the words of Octavio Paz,[1] life is only the mask death wears; the universe, in constant flux, can in no way be trusted, except for (and this with a bitter irony) those appearances which, within the flux, are fixed:

> *Confidence in wickedness, not in the wicked;*
> *in the glass but never in the liquor;*
> *in the corpse, not in the man . . .*
>> (Poem 131)

In another poem, the world—particulated into an apparent delirium—is offered as a list of potencies. Within the body of the poem, words—spiked and pronged—collide; they incise, score, provoke and cross-fertilize each other until, miraculously, a puissant configuration is formed and the disparate atoms have become planets in orbit informing one another's skies, weather and tides. Listen:

> *The Peace, The Whasp, The Shoe Heel . . .*

> *The peace, the whasp, the shoe heel, the slopes,*
> *the dead, the deciliters, the owl,*

---

1. *Threatened by death that is masked and alive* is a line from "Sunstone," Paz's poem that opens with the image of a tree's reflection: *a crystal willow, a poplar of water*—as does Vallejo's "The Book of Nature."

the monstrous and the marvelous

the places, the ringworm, the sarcophagi, the glass, the brunettes,
the ignorance, the kettle, the altarboy,
the drops, the oblivion,
the potentate, the cousins, the archangels, the needle,
the priests, the ebony, the rebuff,
the part, the type, the stupor, the soul . . .

Flexible, saffroned, external, neat,
portable, old, thirteen, bloodsmeared,
those photographed, those ready, those tumescent,
those linked, those long, those beribboned,
        those perfidious . . .

Burning, comparing,
living, raging,
striking, analyzing, hearing, shuddering,
dying, sustaining, settling, crying . . .

Afterward, these, here,
afterward, above,
perhaps, while, behind, so much, so never,
beneath, maybe, distant,
always, that, tomorrow, how much,
how much! . . .

The horrible, the sumptuous, the slowest,
the august, the fruitless,
the ominous, the convulsing, the wet, the fatal,
the whole, the purest, the lugubrious,
the bitter, the satanic, the tactile, the profound . . .
                (Poem 123)

∾

I have mentioned orbits and tides, and indeed, so many of Vallejo's poems observe *processes*—cycles and trajectories of all kinds. The poet's own procedure—which engages a species of nostalgic rage and passionate piercing together of a world in collapse—finds a curious equivalence in the little memory theaters of Joseph Cornell who was also party to cosmic games and Rector of the world's disarticulated bones. Most often Cornell's three-dimensional poems contain those things essential to movement in space: compasses, watches, earth, sun and moon maps, star charts—or they evoke games which rely upon the mastery of projectiles and itineraries such as slot machines, penny arcades and shooting galleries. His *aviaries*—with their mirrors, peepholes and clock springs—fit into this category (because they promise to tell us something about migration) as do his *Observatories* and *Sand Fountains*. Some boxes reveal the workings of wind; others divulge the time of the sun's rising and setting and the exact length of days and nights: another explains the phases of the moon; yet another describes the elements which make up the cosmos. (And Cornell's *Star Hotels* are just that: they offer rooms in space.) A glimpse of one interior gives a peep show's ideal view of a sky bristling with zodiacs. All Cornell's boxes are time machines; they take us into memory's deepest recesses, to those sublime moments of infancy when the world still spelled enchantment. (Think of how Cornell pens in all the mystery of pharaonic Egypt in one small pharmaceutical case!)

Both Vallejo the poet and Cornell the sculptor bid us to *chart further* (and the words belong to Cornell). Both are seized by nostalgia and estrangement; both use fragments in order to create works which—if they instill a profound sensation of flux—are keys to the gates of intuition, works illuminated by that "light which is hardly a mirror's edge from shadow" (Poem 131). And both call upon their own private taxonomies to reorder the world in an intrinsically intuitive and so *organic* way—which explains. in great part, why they are so satisfying.

For example, in Cornell's box entitled *Black Hunter*, the moon's eclipse is explained by a man repeatedly firing a rifle into the sky. This box divulges the secret of an incessant tragedy of mythic proportions: the death of the moon. A tightly closed shell at rest in the box's corner might mirror the mayhem caused by tightly closed minds; however, its presence also implies that the moon, assassinated, is about to be swallowed whole.

Horribly, all this has happened before. The clenched shell is surely digesting an infinity of previously murdered moons.

Again, random objects take on significance because within the box, as within the poem, puissant configurations are formed. The box/poem is a cosmos; the objects within influence one another's trajectories and inform one another with light. Within the box, as within the poem, every single object (or word) has become a reflecting surface.

Just as Vallejo simultaneously demystifies language and gives it back its sacred character, Cornell demystifies matter by containing it in a box with a window—making it visible—and exults it by revealing its secret dimension. Poems and boxes are sacred vessels in which the subtle, the volatile geographies of the spirit are traced in tears and in fire. And in a little box containing a starfish and blue sand, we may read Vallejo's lines:

> *Solar and nutritious Absence of the sea,*
> *and oceanic feeling for everything.*
> (Poem 87)

Cornell described a file he kept on one of his boxes in this way:

> *a diary journal repository laboratory,*
> *picture gallery, museum, sanctuary,*
> *observatory, key . . . the core of a labyrinth,*
> *a learning house for dreams and visions.*
> *It is childhood regained.*

These poems and these boxes, these eroticized and atomized alphabets, this enchantment with the hidden, the broken, the worn, the open, the intact, the tremulous, the murmuring, the silent; this capacity to form a luminous planet of infinite associations from sand, bones, discards and slag, and all the acute pain of losses, is what makes the experience of this art precious and essential.

> *Everything,* Cornell once said, *can be used — but of course one doesn't know it at the time. How does one know what a certain object will tell another?*

Vallejo writes,

> *A pebble, only one, the lowest of all,*
> *controls the whole ill-fated pharaonic sand bank.*
> *The air acquires tension of memories and yearnings,*
> *and under the sun it keeps quiet*
> *until it demands the pyramid's necks . . .*
> *It is time — this advertisement of a great shoestore,*
> *It is time, that marches barefoot*
> *from death toward death.*
>
> (Poem 31)

But, again, death comes only when language seizes up, when, in the words of Vallejo, *men fall, the length of their frozen alphabet, to the ground*

> *And if after so many words,*
> *the word itself does not survive!*
> *If after the wings of the birds,*
> *the standing bird doesn't survive!*
> *It would be much better, really*
> *for them to blow everything, and that's it!*
>
> (Poem 75)

the monstrous and the marvelous

A DREAM

Summer, 1991

In this dream I am a small Italian boy (of the late Renaissance?). My father has taken me to see the workshops that have been set up beneath the arcades of a new palace in the countryside near Naples. Except for the painter's tables, the palace is empty. A beautiful ceiling is in the process of being painted on pieces of fine wood cut into geometrical shapes: hexagons, pentagons, ovals, circles and squares. The paintings are laid out upon the tables and in the torchlight appear to palpitate. I see green lions, a scarlet siren with a scaled tail, sea-scapes, heart-breaking landscapes, the garden of Eden, an entire bestiary! In a blue oval the size and colour of a puffin egg, one perfect human eye gazes at me. And then I see an albino ape falling from a tropical tree, his heart pierced by an arrow. Blood spurts from his wound in thick, crimson ropes. This image is of tremendous potency.

The paintings are all laid out on the floor and varnished. The painters retire and a strange figure appears dressed like a peasant in heavy white cloth, a large grain bag slung over his shoulder. Reaching into his bag he pulls out fistfuls of gold dust with which he "seeds" the wet paintings. Again and again he reaches into his bag for fistfuls of gold. Suddenly the room is filled with particles of gold and I am blinded. I awaken stunned, the sun—flooding the room—is beating against my eyes.

In 1994 I visited the Palazzo del Te in Mántova with Nancy Joyce Peters, who had published the story inspired by my dream: "The Volatilized Ceiling of the Baron Munodi." We were both amazed to see the ceiling I had described. Then I saw a portrait of Federico Gonzaga, the man whose realized dream the palace was. His face was my father's face, exactly.

MANIFESTO IN VOICES

L'homme est descendu du signe.
—Matta

France's Uqbar, the Mas d'Azil in the Pyrénées, was once "truffled" with painted stones. It is supposed that these represent lunar notations. Deeper in the mountains, in the Valley of Marvels, a seemingly infinite number of drawings and engravings—maps, beasts, beings, and moons—animate the rock. These are the embryos of language: *telesma*, perfect things, and the potencies that once served to ignite the imaginations of our most distant ancestors. Europe and Africa, Asia, Australia and Middle America—all our fictions are seeded here, in mountains and in valleys, in such figures painted on stone—visions of the hunt, vivid reveries, barbed wands, red footprints that show the direction a narrative must take, the demons of storms, vulvas self-contained and swollen like bells.

The word is our sign and seal, writes Octavio Paz. *By means of it we recognize each other among strangers (The Labyrinth of Solitude).*

What follows is about recognition, the sacred nature of the word, that *magical ambiguity* (Paz) which gives wings to the beast and meanings to the moon.

Let us imagine something yellow, Borges invites us, *shining, changing. That thing is something in the sky, circular; at other times it has the form of an arc, other times it grows and shrinks. Someone — our common ancestor — gives to that thing the name of moon, different in different languages, and variously lovely (Seven Nights).*

Now it is night (and the voice is George Lamming's, the book: *The Castle of My Skin*); *now it is night with the moon sprinkling its light on everything. The wood is a thick shroud of leaves asleep, and the sleep, like a fog, conceals those who within the wood must keep awake.*

~

Let us imagine that the novel is a species of variable moon and wakeful — its wilderness mapped by Alejo Carpentier, its borderlands plotted by Clarice Lispector, its body dreamed by Severo Sarduy, its atlases bound by Asturias, its circumference squared by Ray Federman, its pantries stocked by Harry Mathews, its songs sung by The Mighty Sparrow, its tigers Borgesian, which — if they can be taught to dance — refuse to carry the cumbersome baggage of orthodoxy. Let us imagine the novel as a kind of *savage beast (that springs upon us) not to rend but to rescue us from death* (W. H. Hudson, *Green Mansions*).

Not long ago the Canadian novelist Barry Callaghan was threatened by a woman (white) who expressed the intention to decock him for having written in a voice other than his own — that of a woman (black). Shortly thereafter, I, too, was aggressed for a similar offense. A character in one of my novels is an Amazonian Indian, something I am not. Next, and within the hour, I witnessed a young writer asking permission of other writers to finish her book:

I am female, heterosexual and white, she said, *yet my novel is narrated by a male homosexual who is Chinese. Do I have the right to continue?*

In answer, I propose these words of Wilson Harris: *I view the novel as a kind of infinite canvas. By infinity I mean that one is constantly breaking down things in order to sense a vision through things. And that applies to characters as well (Kas Kas).*

the monstrous and the marvelous

Like the moon, the novel is a symbol and a necessary reality. Ideally it serves neither gods nor masters. Philosopher's stone, it sublimates, precipitates, and quickens. House of Keys, it opens all our darkest doors. May the Pol Pot Persons of all genders and denominations take heed: to create a fictional world with rigor and passion, to imagine a character of any sex, place, time, or color and make it palpitate and quiver, to catapult it into the deepest forests of our most luminous reveries, is to commit an act of empathy. To write a novel of the imagination is a gesture of tenderness; to enter into the body of a book is a fearless act and generous.

What is forged in the secret act of reading, says Salman Rushdie, *is a different kind of identity, as the reader and writer merge. . . . This "secret identity" . . . is the novel form's greatest and most subversive gift . . . [and] why I elevate the novel above all other forms, why it has always been, and remains my first love: not only is it the art involving the least compromises, but it is also the only one that takes "the privileged arena" of conflicting discourses right inside our heads. The interior space of our imagination is a theatre that can never be closed down (Brick).*

Although it can.

In the Gestapo cellars, George Steiner reminds us (in *Language and Silence*), *stenographers (usually women) took down the noises of fear and agony wrenched, burned, or beaten out of the human voice.* In those cellars, the little stones of potencies, lunar alphabets, rampant bestiaries, and the sacred seeds of recognition were reduced to dirt.

Steiner proposes (as does Alice Miller—one of the lights behind Russell Banks' extraordinary novel *Affliction*) that our century, its great wars, pogroms, and holocausts, are the fulfillment of the previous century's most malignant wishes, an aspiration for perversity and a passion for chaos. It is no accident that the great novels of the 1980s are informed by tragedy, the recognition of finitude, of Total Eclipse. (Again, *Affliction* comes to mind, and *Midnight's Children,* and *Beloved; The Kiss of the Spider Woman* and *Gerald's Party.* . . .)

We have come to the end of a tradition, writes Robert Coover. *I don't*

mean to say that we have come to the end of the novel . . . but that our ways of look-
ing at the world . . . are changing (The Metafictional Muse).

Mystics and physicists alike tell us that moons and tigers—all matter, inert and quickened—are made of the same reeling particles. We move through the maze of the world, and the world's maze moves through us. An intergalactic observer might judge us far less attractive than our cousins the other apes (and it is the baboons, after all, who are blessed with iridescent faces and behinds)—but ours is the species capable of acting with responsibility and an informed heart. Yet, with every volatilized jungle tree (a species that burns its own cannot be expected to respect the lives of plants, to take the time to decode the conversations, perhaps philosophical, of elephants, creatures apparently aware, as are we, of finitude) we prefer to pursue folly, and with an autophageous appetite.

What we ask of writers, says Italo Calvino, *is that they guarantee survival of what we call human in a world where everything appears inhuman.* And he continues: *Literature is like an ear that can hear beyond the understanding of the language of politics (The Uses of Literature).*

I insist: it is not only our right, but our responsibility to follow our imaginations' enchanted paths wherever they would lead us; to heed those voices that inhabit out most secret (and sacred) spaces. When in 1973 thousands were taken to Santiago Stadium to be tortured to death (artists and writers were among the first to be arrested by Pinochet's illegal govemment), Gabriel García Márquez, in an act of defiance and revulsion, ceased to write. After five years, he came to the conclusion that *only by writing could I oppose Pinochet. Without realizing it, I had submitted myself to his censorship (Nouvelle Observateur).*

Literature (and the voice is that of Luisa Valenzuela), *is the site of the cross-waters — the murky and clear waters where nothing is exactly in its place because there is no precise place. We have to invent it each time (Little Manifesto).*

It is precisely this capacity for invention that makes the world worth wanting. The capacity to dream very high dreams and to sing — as did the ancients of Dreamtime — songs potent enough to engender a universe. Those who ask us to deny our dreams would pillage our valley of marvels, would reduce our lunar notations to ashes, would flay our vivid tigers, would deny that the frontiers of the novel, our first love, are infinite.

When we are aware of our disease or hidden motives, writes Italo Calvino, *we have already begun to get the better of them. What matters is the way in which we accept our motives and live through the ensuing crises. This is the only chance we have of becoming different from the way we are — that is the only way of starting to invent a new way of being.*

ACKNOWLEDGMENTS

These essays, or versions of them, originally appeared in the following publications:

"Waking to Eden": from the "Afterword" of *The Jade Cabinet* by Rikki Ducornet (The Dalkey Archive, 1993).

"Optical Terror": from a series of lectures given at the University of Trento, Italy, in the spring of 1994. Sections appear in somewhat different form, under the name Alicia Ombos, in *Phosphor in Dreamland* by Rikki Ducornet (The Dalkey Archive, 1996).

"The Impossible Genus": book review of Rosamond Purcell's *Special Cases: Natural Anomalies and Historical Monsters* (Chronicle Books, 1997), in *Rain Taxi*, Vol. 3, no. 1, Spring 1998.

"On Returning from Chiapas: A Revery in Many Voices": from *The Review of Contemporary Fiction*, "The Future of Fiction," Vol. 16, no 1, Summer 1993.

"Alphabets and Emperors: Reflections on Kafka and Borges": from *Disembodied Poetics*, edited by Anne Waldman and Andrew Schelling (The University of New Mexico Press, 1994).

"Optical Pleasure": from *Rain Taxi*, Vol. 4, no. 1, Spring 1999.

"Haunting by Water": from *The Denver Quarterly*, Vol. 28, no. l., Summer 1993.

"Mapping Paris": a review of *Paris Out of Hand: A Wayward Guide* by Karen Elizabeth Gordan (Chronicle Books, 1996), in *The American Book Review*, Vol. 18, no. 3, April 1997.

"The Monstrous and the Marvelous": from *The American Book Review*, Vol. 19, nos. 5 and 6, July–August and September–October 1998.

"The Death Cunt of Deep Dell": a lecture given at both Elon College and the Naropa Institute, spring and summer 1998. Also in *The Review of Contemporary Fiction*, Vol. 17, no. 3, Fall 1998 and Vol. 14, no. 3, Fall 1994.

"Sortilege": from *Rain Tax*, Vol. 3, no. 3, Winter 1998 / 1999.

"Books of Nature: The Poetry of César Vallejo and the Boxes of Joseph Cornell": from *A Poetics of Criticism*, edited by Juliana Spahr et al.; (Leave Books, 1994). Delivered at the Andean Summit Symposium at the University of Colorado, 1993.

"A Dream": from *The Tiger Garden*, edited by Nicholas Royle (Serpent's Tail, 1996).

"Manifesto in Voices": from *The Novel in the Americas*, edited by Raymond Leslie Williams (University Press of Colorado, 1992). Delivered at The Novel of the Americas Symposium at the University of Colorado, 1991.

∾

The author wishes to extend a special thanks to Giovanna Covi at the University of Trento, Italy.

the monstrous and the marvelous

BIBLIOGRAPHY

Abulafia, Abraham ben Samuel. *The Path of the Names*. Supply city Trigam, 1976.

Acosta, Juvenal, ed. *Light from a Nearby Window: Contemporary Mexican Poetry*. San Francisco: City Lights, 1993.

Baltrušaitis, Jurgis. *Anamorphoses*. Paris: Olivier Perrin, 1995.

Bataille, Georges. *Visions of Excess*. Minneapolis: University of Minnesota, 1985.

Beebe, William, ed. *The Book of Naturalists*. Princeton: Princeton University Press, 1988.

Benítez-Rojo, Antonio. *The Repeating Island*. Trans. James Maraniss. Durham, N.C.: Duke University Press, 1992.

Berkeley, George. *The Works of George Berkeley*. Ed. Alexander Campbell Fraser. Oxford: Clarendon Press.

Blavier, André, ed. *Les Fous Littéraines*. Paris: Henri Veyrier, 1982.

Borges, Jorge Luis. *Seven Nights*. New York: New Directions, 1980.

Borges, Jorge Luis. *Labyrinths*. New York: New Directions, 1962.

Brod, Max. *Franz Kafka: A Biography*. New York: Schocken, 1963.

Cabrera Infante, G. *¡Vaya Papaya!*. Drawings by Ramón Alejandro. Angers, France: Le Polygraphe, 1992.

Caponegro, Mary. *Five Doubts*. New York: Marsilio, 1999.

Carroll, Lewis. *The Complete Works*. The Modern Library. New York: Random House, undated.

Carter, Angela. *The Bloody Chamber*. New York: Penguin, 1987.

———. *Fireworks*. New York: Penguin, 1987.

———. *The Sadeian Woman*. New York: Pantheon, 1979.

———. *Saints and Strangers*. New York: Penguin, 1987.

Caws, Mary Ann. *Joseph Cornell's "Theatre of the Mind."* New York: Thames and Hudson, 1994.

Clarke, Ben, and Clifton Ross, eds. *Voices of Fire: Communiqués and Interviews from the Zapatista National Liberation Army*. Trans. Clifton Ross. Berkeley, Calif.: New Earth, 1994.

Clark, John R. *Form and Frenzy in Swift's Tale of a Tub*. Ithaca, N.Y.: Cornell University Press, 1970.

Cohen, N. Morton. *Lewis Carroll and Alice, 1832–1982*. New York: The Pierpont Morgan Library, 1982.

Cohen, N. Morton. *Reflections in a Looking Glass*. New York: Aperture, 1998.

Coover, Robert. *Briar Rose*. New York: Grove, 1996.

———. *A Night at the Movies*. Normal, 211: Dalkey Archive, 1992.

———. *Pricksongs and Descants*. New York: Penguin, 1970.

Donoso, José. "The Walk" in *Latin American Writers*. Ed. Gabriella Ibieta. New York: St. Martin's Press, 1993.

Ducornet, Rikki. *The Cult of Seizure*. Erin, Ontario: The Porcupine's Quill, 1989.

Fabricant, Carole. *Swift's Landscape*. Baltimore: Johns Hopkins University Press, 1982.

Ferry, David. *Gilgamesh*. New York: Farrar, Straus and Giroux, 1992.

Findlen, Paula. *Possessing Nature*. Berkeley: University of California Press, 1996.

Flaye, Daniel E. *Berkeley's Doctrine of Notions*. New York: St. Martin's Press, 1987.

Flynn, Carol Houlihan. *The Body in Swift and Defoe*. Cambridge: Cambridge University Press, 1990.

Galeano, Edourdo. *Century of the Wind: Memory of Fire III*. Trans. Cedric Belfrage. New York: Pantheon, 1988.

Gander, Forest, ed. *Mouth to Mouth: Poems by Twelve Contemporary Mexican Women*. Minneapolis: Milkweed, 1993.

Gold, Maxwell B. *Swift's Marriage to Stella*. Cambridge: Harvard University Press, 1937.

Gordon, Karen Elizabeth. *Paris Out of Hand (A Wayward Guide)*. San Francisco: Chronicle Books, 1996.

Hinnant, Charles H. *Purity and Defilement in Gulliver's Travels*. New York: St. Martin's Press, 1987.

Johnston, Denis. *In Search of Swift*. Dublin: Hodges Figgis, 1959.

Jonas, Hans. *The Gnostic Religion*. Boston: Beacon Press, 1958.

Kafka, Franz. *Blue Octavo Notebooks*. Trans. Ernst Kaiser and Eithne Wilkins. Cambridge: Exact Change, 1991.

Kafka, Franz. *The Castle*. New York: Schocken Books, 1974.

Kafka, Franz. *The Complete Short Stories*. Trans. Willa and Edwin Muir. New York: Schocken, 1971.

Katzenberger, Elaine, ed. *First World, Ha Ha Ha!* San Francisco: City Lights, 1995.

Kenseth, Joy, ed. *The Age of the Marvelous*. Dartmouth: Hood Museum of Art, 1991.

Kovacs, Maureen Gallery. *The Epic of Gilgamesh*. Stanford: Stanford University Press, 1985.

Las Casas, Bartolomé de. *The Devastation of the Indies*. Trans. Herma Briffault. Baltimore: Johns Hopkins University Press, 1992.

Lauterbach, Ann. *On a Stair*. New York: Penguin, 1997.

Leslie, Shane. *The Skull of Swift*. London: Chatto and Windus, 1928.

Lispector, Clarice. "The Imitation of the Rose" in *Other Fires*. Ed. Alberto Manguel. New York: Potter, 1986.

Mabille, Pierre. *Le Miroir du Merveilleux*. Paris: Editions de Minuit, 1962.

Marcus, Ben. *The Age of Wire and String*. Normal, Ill.: Dalkey Archive, 1997.

Mathews, Harry. *The Conversions*. Normal, Ill.: Dalkey Archive, 1998.

———. *Country Cooking*. Providence, R.I.: The Burning Deck, 1980.

———. *The Journalist*. Normal, Ill.: Dalkey Archive, 1997.

Mawson, Stuart R. *Diseases of the Ear*. London: Edward Arnold, 1963.

McShine, Kynaston. Ed. *Joseph Cornell*. New York: Museum of Modern Art, 1980.

Monegal, E. Rodriguez. *Borges*. Seville: Ecrivains de toujours, 1970.

Murray, J. Middleton. *Jonathan Swift*. London: Cape, 1954.

Past, Ambar. *The Sea on Its Side*. Trans. Jack Hirschman. Sausalito: Post-

Apollo, 1994.

Pitcher, George, ed. *The Philosophy of George Berkeley*. New York: Garland, 1989.

Popol Vuh. Trans. Dennis Tedlock. New York: Simon & Schuster/Touchstone, 1985.

Purcell, Rosamond. *Special Cases: Natural Anomalies and Historical Monsters*. San Francisco: Chronicle Books, 1997.

Purcell, Rosamond Wolff, and Stephen Jay Gould. *Finder's Keepers*. New York: W. W. Norton, 1992.

Sade, Marquis de. *The 120 Days of Sodom*. New York: Grove, 1966.

Sandars, N. K. *The Epic of Gilgamesh*. London: Penguin, 1960.

Scholem, Gershom G. *On the Kabala and its Symbolism*. New York: Schocken, 1965. .

Shesgreen, Sean. *Engravings by Hogarth*. New York: Dover, 1973.

Swift, Jonathan. *The Complete Poems*. Ed. Pat Rogers. Ithaca: Yale University Press, 1983.

———. *The Correspondence*. Ed. F. Elrington Bell. London: G. Bell and Sons, 1910.

———. *A Tale of a Tub*. Oxford: Oxford University Press, 1958.

———. *The Prose Works*. Ed. Herbert Davis. 14 Vols. Oxford: Oxford University Press, 1939–1968.

Vallejo, César. *The Complete Posthumous Poetry*. Trans. Clayton Eshelman. Berkeley: University of California Press, 1980.

Waldman, Diane. *Joseph Cornell*. New York: George Braziller, 1977.

Williams, Harold, ed. *Journal to Stella*. Vol. II. Oxford: Clarendon Press, 1963.

Xue, Can. *The Embroidered Shoes*. New York: Henry Holt, 1997.

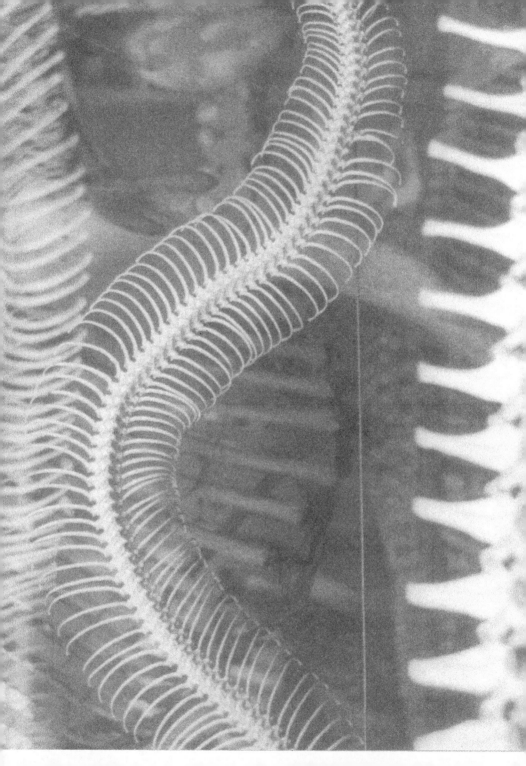

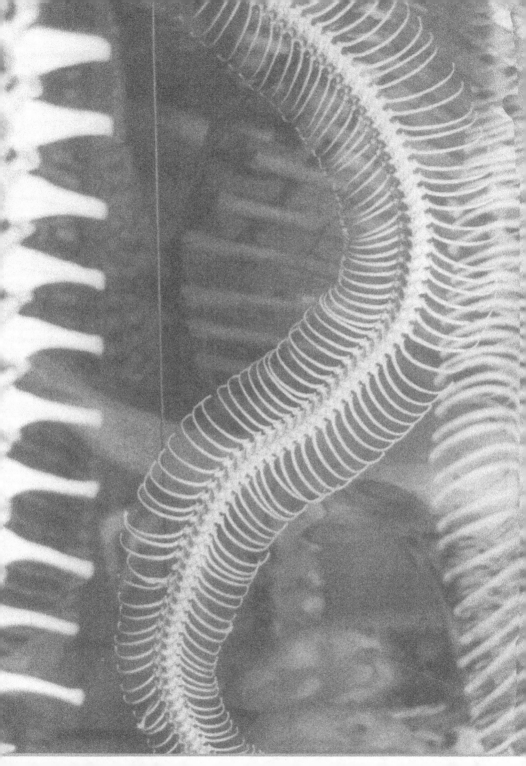

Printed in the USA
CPSIA information can be obtained
at www.ICGtesting.com
JSHW082213140824
68134JS00014B/607